A Student's Brain:

The Parent/Teacher

Manual

A
Brains.org
Publication

Copyright ©2003 by Kathie F. Nunley, EdD

Parts of this book were previously published in *The Regular Educator's Guide to the Brain* ©1999, 2000, 2001, by K. F Nunley.

ISBN 1-929358-11-3

Additional copies of this book as well as all books by Kathie F Nunley and support are available at:
Brains.org
&
Help4Teachers.com
54 Ponemah Road,
Amherst, NH 03031
(603)249-9521
Email: Kathie@brains.org

Cover Design by Micheal R. Eudy
Eudy Animation Dallas, Texas

Printed in the USA by Morris Publishing
3212 East Highway 30
Kearney, NE 68847

Books by Kathie F. Nunley

~~ **Layered Curriculum:** *The practical solution for teachers with more than one student in their classroom.*

~~ **Layered Curriculum:** *The workbook.*

~~**A Student's Brain**: *The parent/teacher manual.*

~~ **The Regular Educator's Guide to Special Ed.**

~~ **Keegan**: *Looking at the world through Autism.*

Available at: http://Help4Teachers.com

Foreword

This book has come as a result of your requests for a written version of my Brain Biology workshop material. I designed it to be just that, conversational in tone, and complete with my obligatory little sketches. The sketches are not designed to be anatomically correct nor should you consider relative size in interpreting them. More exact pictures can be found in any good physiology or bio-psychology textbook.

Parts of this book were previously published in *The Regular Educator's Guide to the Brain* ©1999,2000.2001, Kathie F Nunley.

This book is dedicated to my four children.

*For **Keegan**, who gave me an education in Autism.*
*For **Kahlia** who gave me an education in Traumatic Brain Injury and recovery.*
*For **Keller** who gave me an education in Dyslexia.*
*And for **Kole** who gave me an education in Miracles.*

Preface

Nearly everywhere we look today, we find the term"brain-based education" or brain-based learning."

Why have people suddenly become obsessed with the brain? The fact is, that we as humans have learned more, in the last decade or two, about how this amazing organ operates, than we have in the entire history of mankind.

Educators and parents are particularly interested in all this new research because it makes our jobs so much easier as we learn to be more effective. And what we are learning is causing those of us in education to re-think the way we deliver instruction.

We are finding out that the brain doesn't always work in the ways we assumed it did. Some of the new information is validating old beliefs, some is re-shaping new beliefs, but all of it is fascinating.

Nothing entertains the human brain more than the study of the human brain.

Table of Contents

Chapter Eleven

Appendix A :

Appendix B:

Glossary

Selected References

Index

Additional Books - Order Page

Chapter one

The Basic Structure and Function of a Neuron

In order to understand how our students' and our own brains function, we need to start with some basic understanding about nerves. After all, the brain is basically just a large organized wad of nerves held together with a bit of "glue".

And so we start with the basic structure and function of a nerve and its basic component, the nerve cell. The brain is primarily a collection of these uniquely shaped and specialized body cells called **neurons**. Here is a neuron:

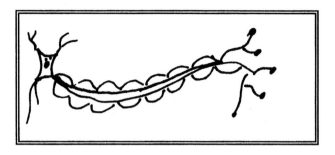

Before we venture into the complex neuron activity within the brain, let's first examine how these neurons work in the relatively simple **peripheral nervous system** (PNS). The PNS includes the area outside of our brain and spinal cord. These are our body nerves.

If I were to drop a hammer on your toe, it would appear to you that you feel the pain in your toe. But in reality you are feeling the pain in your brain. The information of the attack must begin in your toe and travel up to your brain in order for you to interpret the sensation as pain and then send a corresponding response back down to your foot (probably some type of response aimed at me and involving a great deal more than just your foot too.)

This information travels via nerves. But the term *nerve* may be a little misleading. Nerves are not long stringy things like threads. They are actually hundreds of thousands of neurons like the one above, lined up end to end, nearly touching. The sequence appears like this:

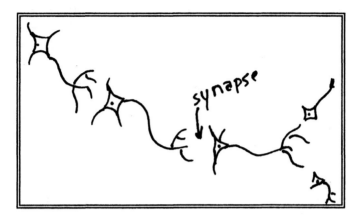

Notice that the neurons do not actually touch each other. They are separated by a space, called a **synapse** or synaptic junction. This space, or synapse is actually the most important part of the nervous system because what goes on inside this space is the key to how the entire system functions.

Neurons communicate with each other using two basic methods - one electrical and one chemical. To explain, let's go back to my dropping the hammer on your toe. Before the hammer drops, the neurons in your toe were sitting there, minding their own business in what is called a **resting state**.

The cell is resting because no great electrical exchange is occurring. When it is resting, positive electrical charges outside the neuron are kept separate from the negative charge inside the neuron by the cell membrane. Everything is at peace as seen here:

However, once the hammer drops, the whole scenario changes. The force of the hammer has now "stimulated" the neuron.

You can stimulate nerve cells in four different ways which is what allows us to have so many different senses. You can stimulate a neuron by touching it or heating it(our sense of hearing and touch), putting chemicals on it(our taste and smell) or shining light on it (our sight).

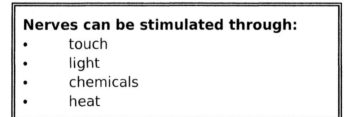

Nerves can be stimulated through:
- touch
- light
- chemicals
- heat

By doing one of these things, you cause the cell membrane to let down its guard. It now becomes permeable and the positive and negative charges no longer have anything to separate them. Small holes in the membrane open, and the positive charges rush in to meet the negative charges and viola', electricity. The electrical charge quickly moves down the length of the neuron until it gets to the end of the cell branches. This is referred to as an **action potential.** Action potential is just a fancy term for "firing" the nerve.

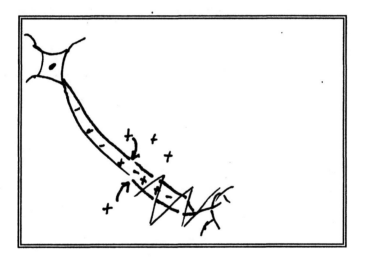

The electricity that moves down the length of a neuron is similar to the electricity we are all familiar with as household current. The only real difference is the speed. Our body's electricity runs at a much slower speed (3,000 meters/second) than household current (300,000,000 meters/second). You may have noticed this speed difference is you've ever tried to plug your body wiring into the household current!

Some of our neurons are covered with a fatty covering, called a **myelin sheath**. These so called myelinated neurons can transmit electricity up to ten times faster than non-myelinated neurons. It is this myelin sheath that accounts for the white and gray matter in our brain. White matter is made up of the myelinated neurons. Gray matter are the plain variety. (Fat is somewhat white in color).

Chemical Communication

Whether the nerve cell is myelinated or not, they communicate in much the same way.   When the electricity reaches the end of the neuron it needs to somehow "tag" the next neuron.   Neurons relay the information to the next neuron in a chemical fashion. So, at this point, the communication becomes chemical in nature.

At the end of each nerve cell, sacs of chemicals are sitting and waiting to be released into the synapse. These chemicals are called **neurotransmitters.** The electrical impulse causes the chemicals to be released as it reaches the end of the neuron. The chemicals then are free to move across the synapse, bump into the next neuron and cause it to fire its own electrical impulse. Remember that chemicals are one of the things that will excite or "fire" a neuron. Now the message has once again becomes electrical in nature, traveling down this new nerve cell until it reaches the end and releases its own supply of neurotransmitters, and so on and so on and so on.

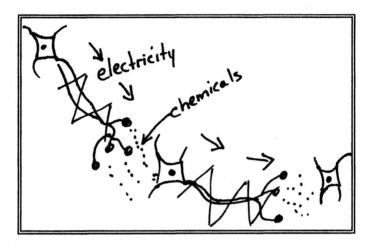

Although we will see that there are dozens of different neurotransmitters at work in our central nervous system, the peripheral nervous system primarily uses only two. Regardless of the type though, neurotransmitters work in one of two ways. They either speed up or slow down the speed in which one neuron communicates with another.

If the neurotransmitter belongs to the group that speeds up communication, we call it an **agonist**. An agonist excites or fires another neuron upon contact. If the neurotransmitter belongs to the group that slows down communication it is called an **antagonist**. An antagonist inhibits or prevents the firing of another neuron. It generally does this by blocking **receptor sites** on the next neuron. Receptor sites are the places on a nerve cell where the neurotransmitters can attach.

If you think of a key and lock system, the receptor site is the lock and the neurotransmitter is the key that fits into it to open the door. Antagonist neurotransmitters would act similar to gum stuffed in the keyhole.

If today is a good day for you and you are feeling quite chipper, alert and ready to go and do, then you probably have a surplus of one of the agonists. Perhaps that doesn't describe your day. Maybe you are instead, feeling rather lethargic, depressed and generally not ready to go and do anything. If that's the case, then your nervous system is probably running on too much antagonist.

The agonists cause the message between one neuron and another to move quickly. Messages travel fast and sensations are more intense. Antagonists slow down communication, and information and sensations are less intense.

It should be apparent that in order to have a nice emotionally stable life, one needs to have a good balance between agonist neurotransmitters and antagonists. You can see that too much of one type might make you so hyper and manic that you can't focus and get anything done during the day. On the other hand, too much of the other would make you so lethargic and depressed that you can barely fall out of bed and get anything done. So for the most part, they stay in a fairly good balance. Oh, you may have some good days and some not so good, but they balance fairly well.

But just in case you had this thought upon rising today, *"Gee, I'm just not happy with my neurotransmitter levels today,"* you are in luck. Humans learned long ago that we could make or find, in nature, chemical mimics of neurotransmitters to ingest. This way, if you didn't like the overall mood Mother Nature provided, you could use chemical mimics to make adjustments.

One of the most common of these mimics is **caffeine**. Caffeine works by getting into your nervous system and acting like an agonistic neurotransmitter. Under the influence of caffeine, messages move quicker between neurons, perceptions are more intensified and even learning is increased when caffeine is used in moderation. It may occur to you that most of us who use caffeine have never really grasped that term *moderation* and that leads to an entirely new situation.

Nerves cells, like most components of your body, have a biological drive for **homeostasis**, or sameness. The body doesn't like things out of balance and has all sorts of procedures to maintain and restore balance. It is this need for homeostasis which causes us so much trouble as we will see throughout this book.

Here is our first example. Because the body adjusts for the imbalance, once we start providing an artificial neurotransmitter (in this case, caffeine) on a regular basis, our nervous system quits making it. Basically my neurons say to themselves, *"why should we bother making this stuff? If we just wait a few minutes she'll dump a pot of coffee in here and we're off and running!"* And now I have a physical addiction to caffeine.

So if you are physically addicted to caffeine, what that means is you have been providing it to your nerves for so long and on such a regular basis that your nerve cells have come to depend upon you doing so and they have ceased making their own supply - or at least significantly reduced their production.

A caffeine addiction can be a real struggle for anyone trying to withdraw. But if you quit using caffeine, your body should start producing its own neurotransmitter once again after a couple of weeks.

On a related note however, we are also currently looking at the significant issue of caffeine addiction in the United States. We now have our first fully grown population who has been raised on chronic use of artificial neurotransmitters, through our soft-drink industry. A couple of generations ago, parents didn't give caffeine to children. It was considered an adult product and there was somewhat of a cultural taboo about children and caffeine. Today that cultural taboo has vanished.

Many parents today think nothing of offering caffeine to children at a very young age and on a very regular basis. Why most of us have seen children drinking caffeinated soft drinks right in the baby bottle. Many researchers theorize that our sudden increase in attention deficit disorder and hyperactivity which lingers longer than normal might be blamed on this practice of regular artificial neurotransmitter use during the first 12 years of life.

For it is during the first 12 years that the central nervous system is coming into maturity. It is possible that the regular use of artificial neurotransmitters (ie: caffeine) during this time period can interfere with the nervous system's ability to produce and regulate these things naturally.

The problem tends to be limited to the United States as we are one of the few countries that allows soft drink manufacturers to add caffeine to their product. While cola based drinks naturally contain some caffeine, the other products are intentionally caffeinated. For example, when I buy a Mountain Dew in Canada there is no caffeine in it. Only American Mountain Dew is caffeinated.

This has grown to be a problem weighing heavily on our public education system as well because of the increasing presence of soft drink concession machines in our public schools. It is rare to go into any public school these days, coast to coast, and not find concession machines as a major funding source for the school. While nearly all high schools have these machines, the middle school numbers are growing and now nearly half of all elementary school have some type of concession machine available for students.

caffeine amounts in common products

1 cup of coffee	135 mgs.
Cup of Ben & Jerry's coffee frozen yogurt	85 mgs.
1 Excedrin tablet	65 mgs
can of Mountain Dew	56 mgs.
1 cup of tea	50 mgs
Can of Diet Coke	47 mgs.
Can of Sunkist Orange	42 mgs.
Can of Dr Pepper	42 mgs
Can of Pepsi	38 mgs.
Can of Coke	35 mgs.
Cup of green tea	30 mgs.
1 Hershey Dark Chocolate Bar	31 mgs.
1 Hershey Bar	10 mgs.
Cup of cocoa	5 mgs

If the caffeine issue isn't enough to warrant a re-look, then the research on calcium loss should be. In addition to the problems of caffeine, carbonated soft drinks are known to pull the calcium out of bones which is particularly bothersome to girls. In fact, adolescent girls who consume soft drinks are 3 times as likely to break a bone as adolescent girls who do not.

On the opposite side of caffeine use, we also have recreational substances that mimic the antagonist neurotransmitters and slow our nervous systems down. The most popular one of these would be alcohol. Alcohol has many actions in the body as we will see later, but its primary action in the peripheral nervous system is as an artificial antagonist.

If you put alcohol into your body, it works by going into the space between neurons, and slowing down transmission of information. In fact if I put enough alcohol into your body I could probably drop a hammer on your toe all day long and you wouldn't care. This is because alcohol can actual be a nerve "blocker".

Nerve-blockers do just like the name suggests, they block transmission between neurons. There are major, general nerve-blockers such as morphine and very specific nerve-blockers such as novocaine, like your dentist uses. Even aspirin, to some extent, is a nerve blocker and that is how it is able to reduce pain.

So, alcohol works by mimicking a neurotransmitter which slows down how fast neurons communicate. Under the influence of alcohol, responses are slower, perceptions less intense, and with enough alcohol you really wouldn't notice the hammer I dropped on your toe.

Many recreational drugs work by mimicking a particular neurotransmitter and either slow down or speed up the communication in the neural synapses.

Hyperactivity

One of the reasons that I even address neurotransmitters in the peripheral nervous system is that we see a problem in these in that disorder you may have heard about, called **attention deficit/hyperactivity disorder** (ADHD). Attention deficit disorder and Hyperactivity disorder are really two completely different disorders. We do a disservice to them both by lumping them together and calling it ADHD.

Attention deficit disorder is a problem in the brain, which we'll look at shortly. It is rarely, if ever, outgrown. Hyperactivity on the other hand is a problem outside of the brain. It is a problem in the peripheral nervous system. **Hyperactivity disorder** is almost always outgrown.

The vast majority of children with Hyperactivity disorder outgrow it by age 9. It peaks between age 7 and 8 and then wanes from there. So if you have a 7 year old with hyperactivity, this is as bad as things are probably going to get.

It seems logical to most people that children with hyperactivity disorder have a problem with neurotransmitters. But it comes as a surprise to most people that the direction of the imbalance seems counterintuitive. Though children with hyperactivity disorder look like they make too much agonist neurotransmitters, in reality they do not make enough. Children with hyperactivity have an underactive nervous system. Yes, I wrote *underactive*. Their nervous systems run slow. Communication between neurons is not as fast and it is in you and I (supposing we do not have hyperactivity disorder)

At first glance, this may not make sense. It conflicts with what you might think, because the hyperactive child appears to be moving too fast, be too impulsive. It might make more sense to you if you thought for a minute about a time in your life when you were really tired and you were trying to keep yourself going.

A good example is one most of us are familiar with. You are driving home late at night, and are getting very sleepy, but you are trying to make it home, or at least to the next interstate exit. What types of things do you do?

Interestingly, most of us do very similar antics. We turn on the radio, and sing (loudly). We turn up the air-conditioner or open a window. Many of us snack on something. The next step generally involves shoulder kinesthetics. The workout may even become aerobic in nature. If it gets bad enough we may even slap ourselves in the face, pinch ourselves, dig our fingernails into our hands, and jump around in our seat. Most everyone is familiar with that little "gotta stay awake while driving tired" dance. So there you are driving down the freeway with the wind blowing your hair, singing at the top of your lungs and slapping yourself in the face.

What you have now is the hyperactive child. These kids are trying to "wake up" their nervous system. It is running too slow. Those impulsive, erratic behaviors we see in our classroom are often a "gotta stay alert while sitting in class" dance. For this reason, hyperactivity is often treated with stimulant medication. By revving up their nervous system, the children can now focus their attention on what they should and the impulsive behaviors decrease.

As we will see later, there are other areas of the nervous system to blame for the attention deficit which often comes with hyperactivity disorder.

Chapter Two

The Central Nervous System-- Lower Brain

So much for the peripheral or body nervous system. Now let's look at the even larger system - the **central nervous system (CNS).** The central nervous system or CNS is much more complicated than the peripheral nervous system. For one thing, it uses a lot more neurotransmitters. Not only does it use the two main PNS system chemicals, **norepinephrine** and **epinephrine**, but it uses major chemicals such as **Dopamine, Serotonin**, **Acetylcholine** and a host of others. In fact, some estimate there may be as many as 90 or more different neurotransmitters at work in the CNS.

Besides the numbers of neurotransmitters, another issue which makes the CNS so complex is that different neurotransmitters have different actions in different parts of the brain. For example, if you are low on serotonin in one area of the brain then you have depression. But if you are missing serotonin in another part of your brain now you have obsessive-compulsive disorder. You can see how this makes it very difficult for the pharmaceutical industry as it tries to make treatments for various mental illnesses.

Major neurotransmitters and their actions

neurotransmitter	involved in:
norepinephrine	arousal, alertness, memory
epinephrine	involved in fight/fligh resonse
serotonin	sleep, mood, appetite
dopamine	pleasure, learning, memory
gamma-aminobutyric acid	(GABA) motor activity, sleep
Endorphins	learning, memory, pleasure

See Appendix B for more information on neurotransmitters.

The Spinal Cord

One of the most important issues that has come out of brain imaging studies is the reminder that the CNS is more than just the brain. In fact, it has two main parts, the brain AND **the spinal cord.**

You remember your spinal cord, don't you? You probably learned about it in the third grade when a teacher taught you "your Central Nervous System is composed of your brain and your spinal cord." And you've probably not given much thought to it since then.

One of the significant issues that has come out of brain imaging studies in the last two decades has been the notion that we have grossly underestimated the power of our spinal cord and other lower regions of the central nervous system. While most teachers and parents may consider the spinal cord to be something completely unrelated to school, education and learning, it appears that this lower region of the CNS actually causes us many of the frustrations we have in education.

So, let's take a look at that spinal cord. What does it do? We all have one. Someone once told us not to sever ours, so it must be doing something important. But what? The spinal cord has three main functions, the three R's. Reflexes, relay, and routine tasks.

You are probably familiar with the first two functions. Reflexes are those life and death issues of survival where we don't want to waste time decision making. So they come pre-wired into our body system with an automatic muscle/motor response in the spinal cord. This way, when you touch a hot stove, you can instantly remove your hand rather than wait for the brain to weigh all the available options at the expense of your fingers and skin.

The second spinal cord function, relay, is most likely the one you learned at an earlier age. Someone told you that the spinal cord relays information between body nerves and the brain. That is indeed an important function, and probably the main reason for you not to sever the thing. It is of critical importance that your brain know what is going on in the rest of the body. You certainly can damage the spinal cord and survive, but if you were to completely sever it, life would cease.

Main Functions of the Spinal Cord:
•   reflexes •   relay information between brain & body •   routine tasks

It is the third function, routine tasks, that I'd like to call your attention to. Routine tasks are handled at a spinal cord level. This actually is quite handy, for in reality, your brain doesn't do anything very well. Let me repeat, *your brain doesn't do anything with any grace, polish or finesse.* In fact, if you really want something messed-up, ask your brain to handle it for you.

Human brains are good at one task - learning new material and activities. There is nothing better on the face of this earth for discovering, problem solving, comparing and reasoning new information. However, once a task is learned, it uses smaller and smaller regions of the brain's cortex as many aspects of the activity are shunted down to lower regions, including the spinal cord. It is at this point that the activity begins to look good. It has polish, routine, and is generally done well.

One of the best examples for this is to look at the activity of walking. Many of us are familiar with a youngster learning to walk. It may be cute, but let's face it, it does not look good. There appears to be little grace, poise, and finesse. The poor thing stumbles, wobbles, and doesn't say upright for very long. This is your brain walking. It doesn't do it well.

As you began to master the art of walking, your brain became more efficient in the use of brain circuitry, used smaller and smaller regions of the cortex and moved a large part of the activity down to your spinal cord. Fortunately your brain had the good sense to relegate the job to an area that could do it well and more importantly, free your brain's cortex up for other activities - like thinking.

In addition to not doing something well, your brain's cortex can only work with one thing at a time. So a young child can either walk or think, but not both. You, on the other hand can - because the walking has become a spinal cord activity. Today, most of us can walk down the hall and plan our summer vacation at the same time. If you can walk down the hall and plan your summer vacation simultaneously, then one of those jobs is handled by your spinal cord.

What else can the spinal cord do? Why, it can drive your car! Have you ever driven to work, shut the car off in the parking lot and thought, "Wow, I sure hope all those lights were green, because I have no memory of getting here this morning". If so, then that tells you that your spinal cord was driving your car. Isn't that wonderful. If your spinal cord was driving, what was your brain doing? Probably planning your summer vacation.

In fact, most of us really appreciate all the routine tasks that can be handled at that level, because it does in fact free our brain up for thinking. Many of us do our best thinking during long periods of spinal cord activities. I've solved many a problem in the shower or during a long solo highway drive.

Often times we get frustrated when a task we truly mean to be handled at the brain's cortex level, in fact gets handled at the spinal cord level. A good example here is reading. Have you ever read something with your spinal cord? Probably. It's very frustrating. We've all experienced that frustration of reading a whole page of something, getting to the bottom and having to start all over again because we have no idea of what we just read. It sure looked like we were reading. Our eyes were moving from word to word down the page, but our brain was on a different task.

Most of us can scan across the page, process the phonetics of words at a very primitive level, while planning our summer vacation or working on an important issue. In fact, it is important that those eye muscle movements and phonetic processing be handled by lower regions of our brain. That's what allows for comprehension of the passage. If you cannot get through the phonetics and physical act of reading at lower brain levels, then you would read like most first graders.

A first grader takes a long time to read a passage and more importantly, has little or no comprehension of their reading. This is because for them, the physical act of reading and sounding out the words is a cortical (using the brain's cortex) activity. You and I are much more efficient at it, which then allows our cortex to do one of two things - either comprehend what we are reading, or plan our summer vacation.

And yet how many of us teach or parent much older children who still read where the physical act of reading and sounding out the words is such a cortical activity that there is no functional comprehension to their reading. Unfortunately there are many children, much older than 6, who still read where the de-coding part of reading is a major brain activity. In fact, Reid Lyon, head of the National Institute of Child Development was recently quoted as saying that today, 45% of the United States' 9-year-olds are reading-disabled. Forty-five percent! That is inexcusable in a nation with as many resources as ours.

How can this happen? The research is pointing to a variety of causes. One of them is that reading programs today are generally packaged by publishing houses and sold to school districts. They come with a large price tag, so most districts just invest in *one*. There is the problem. Even the best reading program available is only going to be successful with about 50% of children. So, without a variety of instructional practices, many children do not learn to read well in the early grades.

Another significant issue is that we allow for a wide variation in normal development in all aspects of human development, except academics. We allow for a large range of "normal" development for things like learning to speak clearly, learning to walk, entering puberty, natural death, etc. However, when it comes to academics, we forget that differences in readiness exist. And sometimes these differences can be significant.

There is no research to support the practice of teaching reading to ALL 6 year-olds. Not all 6 year old brains are ready to read. Many were ready much earlier. But because our schools have become large institutions, with all the restrictions attached, we ask all students regardless of background, gender, or cortex development to learn to read at age 6. And what happens to the little brain who's window is open in another year or two or three? By then, they're in the third grade and the curriculum has moved on. We never go back and catch the child when they, personally are ready to read. And so they are often left behind.

Mindless School Work

But let's move back to the "mindless" act of reading I mentioned earlier. When you sit in bed and read at night but your mind is working on problems of the day, we all know what little comprehension is gleaned from the reading. And that is my next point.

Spinal cords and lower brain regions can do lots of things. In fact they do most of the daily, nitty-gritty tasks in our lives. If you can do *task X* while planning your summer vacation, then *task X* is a spinal cord activity. Now that we understand this, you may be able to see how often children and students are putting things at this level when in fact we intend them to be at a much higher level.

The biggest place of concern for this is in the classroom. Too much valuable instructional time in the classroom is spent working student's spinal cords when that is often not the intent of the teachers. Do you know children who can do their homework in front of the television and tell you everything about the show? Do you know children who can do their schoolwork while chatting on-line, talking on the phone, visiting with a friend? We all do.

One of the biggest issues we face in education is moving students out of their spinal cord for day-to-day activities. One of my personal favorite spinal cord activities is copying glossary definitions out of the back of the textbook. I think most of us could complete that activity while planning our summer vacation? Look at other types of school work. Can students watch a video, fill out a worksheet, copy notes off the board, even 'read' the textbook while planning their week-end social calendar? Of course they can, and they do.

This is not to say that looking up glossary words, reading a text, completing worksheets and other traditional types of school activities are not valuable ways of instruction. In fact, these can all be excellent ways of learning material, IF the student's attention is focused on the task.

My point here is that if our instructional objective is not to exercise the spinal cord of our students, then we had better do something to ensure the focus of attention while doing school work.

> Millions of items of the outward order are present to my senses which never properly enter into my experience. Why? Because they have no interest for me. My experience is what I agree to attend to. Only those items which I notice shape my mind. - William James (1890). *Principles of Psychology*.

If the child is not attending to the task, then no learning will be taking place. When I designed **Layered Curriculum**™ for the classroom, one of the key reasons for oral defense is to help ensure that day-to-day school and homework are handled at higher regions of the brain rather than the spinal cord.

One of the easiest ways to ensure that students are attending to the day-to-day activities is to hold them accountable for learning the material rather than just "doing" the assignment. The Layered Curriculum™ model is based on the argument that classroom instruction and policy have too much focus on the process and not enough on the product. There is nothing wrong with asking a student if she did the homework. But we sometimes forget to also ask her if she learned from the homework.

You may also begin to see here some problems we have with children, especially adolescents, in that they do not have the experience necessary to perform some routine activities at the spinal cord level. As an example, look at driving. Have you seen a 16 year old lately driving a car? Does that look good? Is there any grace, poise, finesse to that? That is a brain driving a car. Brains really are not very good at things. There is no mastery.

One of the reasons adults are concerned about 16 year-olds driving cars with friends is that you are now asking them to do two brain activities simultaneously and it can't be done. They can either drive the car or talk to their friends, but not both at the same time without disastrous results. Until driving because routine, drivers are safest alone in the car or at least without such distractions as peers. (Many adults are reminded of this same issue regarding cell phone use while driving)

The Hind Brain

Let us move up a little higher in the central nervous system and actually venture into the brain proper. The first swelling we come to is a region called the **hind brain**. In biology we often refer to this as the fish brain because it is the part of the brain we share with fish. It is a very primitive region of the brain and performs functions basic to the survival of the animal.

In other words, it runs our body. The hind brain makes sure your heart stays beating and that you breathe. It is involved in the regulation of sleep and sleep cycles. During dreaming, an area in this region paralyzes your muscles so that you don't act out on your dreams. (In many children and some adults, this part doesn't do its job well which results in sleepwalking, sleep talking, etc.)

Hind Brain:
- Medulla
- Pons

However, there is one area in this region that we will focus on, primarily because of the important role it plays in the classroom. It is a region known as the **Reticular Activating System (RAS)**. The RAS is responsible for screening all the sensory information that is coming into your brain at any given moment and establishing a priority for the processing of that information. This is the region that chooses what you are paying attention to at any given moment in time.

Sorting the important from the unimportant is no small task. Vast quantities of sensory information are available to us at any given moment. Right now, as you read this, your brain is bombarded with a great deal of sensory input - most of which goes unnoticed. At this moment, what can you hear? What can you taste? Smell? What about visual information. How many objects, shapes and colors are in your visual field right now? What about your sense of touch - can you feel your shoes, socks, shirt, watch band, or even the hair coming out of your head?

Thank goodness we don't pay attention to all of that at once. Thanks to our RAS. That's its job. Basically the RAS filters all this information, sorts the important from the unimportant and channels our attention. This ability to ignore the unimportant items is referred to as **habituation**. It is a vital part of maintaining sanity and the inability to habituate to some stimuli has been blamed for all sorts of mental distresses.

So what helps cue this region in as to what is important? It has three or four big priorities and there is a bit of a hierarchy to it all. The biggest priority for the area is physical need. The physical needs of the body will always get attention which is why it is very difficult to watch television when on a strict diet. It seems like all the commercials are for food and you notice every one. It is also the reason that it is difficult to take a nature hike with a pebble in your shoe. One of life's biggest distractions for me is the tag in the back of a shirt which sometimes has a little corner on it that pokes me all day long. If you've ever experienced that sensation you know how distracting it can be.

It is difficult to teach anything to a student who has a physical need which has not been met. If that child is hungry, if they have to go to the bathroom, if they have a blister on their hand, it will be an overriding priority for their attention.

Priorities of the RAS:
(1) physical needs
(2) novelty
(3) self-made choice

The second priority of the RAS is novelty. Something novel, new, or out of the norm will always catch your attention. This is the reason you can drive home at the end of the day and not know how you got home but know you didn't hit someone or some thing. If you had hit something, that would have been novel and you would have noticed it.

Novelty is also the reason students listen to teachers at the beginning of the year - we are novel. That's called the *"honeymoon period"*. How long do you think the honeymoon lasts? For many of us, not long. By spring, the student is sitting in class wondering what is more important, the sound of the teacher's voice or the feel of his shoes on his feet.

The third big priority of the RAS is self-made choice. That's just our conscious mind deciding, for whatever reason, that we want to pay attention to something. Perhaps my favorite basketball team is playing for the last shot in a close game so I pay attention. Basically, I make a decision that this game is important to me and I'm going to ignore all the other events and issues going on around me and pay attention to the game.

Shocking as it may be, in the classroom, that's what we teachers are banking on. We are counting on students to come into our room, make a conscious decision that *"Geometry is important to me. I'm going to ignore all the other things going on around me today and pay close attention to the teacher because I've always wanted to learn about the Pythagorean theorem."*

Shocking? Yes, but truthful, because unless you are feeding starving children or wearing a different clown suit each day for novelty, there is not a lot more to go on for attention.

There is one other item that will catch a person's attention and that is the sound of her name. By around 18 months, your name is fairly well wired into your RAS and rarely do we habituate to it. This leads to an interesting issue referred to as the **cocktail-party phenomenon**. Let's say you are in a crowded room talking to your best friend. Suddenly, from across the room, your name comes up in someone else's conversation. Do you hear it? You bet you do. Now your mind stops all other activity as you focus your attention on that conversation across the room.

A person rarely can tune out the sound of her name, but it is difficult to use this approach for gaining attention for any long period of time as it tends to irrate the person due to the fact that they cannot habituate to it.

In fact you can exhaust a person and basically drive them crazy by just inserting their name into every sentence throughout the day. By the end of the day they might very well feel just like a classroom teacher.

Teachers, you know how tired you are at the end of the day. It's not because you have been lifting weights and running track all day. It's because you have never gotten any mental "down" time. Every time you try to head off into some nice fantasy or daydream, some little darling calls your name and back you come. You are mentally tired from being attentive all day long. Everyone needs a little mental down time to rest and rejuvenate.

The RAS is a great brain region - when it works. By age 7 it should be fairly mature and fully functioning. It is supposed to work 24 hours a day, 7 days a week and in most of us, works even while we are asleep. This is the reason most of us don't wet the bed anymore, and the reason a new mother or father can sleep through the neighbors coming and going all night, but wake to the small rustle of blankets moving in the crib down the hall.

If the RAS doesn't work at all, then you have schizophrenia. People with schizophrenia have a very difficult time filtering the important from the unimportant. You can see how uncomfortable life would be if all sensory input came in with the same priority and you were unable to filter it.

If the RAS works, but just not very well, then you have Attention Deficit Disorder (ADD). People with ADD have very limited blood flow in this particular region of the brain. The dopamine receptors in this area are dysfunctional, the area is inefficient and it shows up in blood flow measures.

Actually there are two main areas of the brain affected by attention deficit disorder. The first and biggest area effected is the RAS, but a second brain region is also involved, known as the **pre-frontal cortex**. The pre-frontal cortex is located much higher up in the brain, right behind the forehead. The pre-frontal cortex is involved in decision making and we will see its role in a later chapter.

Unlike its frequent partner-in-crime, hyperactivity disorder, ADD is frequently a life long condition. One of the problems we have in linking attention deficit to hyperactivity is that people often times make the inaccurate assumption that once the hyperactivity has disappeared, so has the attention deficit and that is generally not the case at all. ADD can be treated with behavioral interventions as well as medications which adjust the dopamine levels in this region. The most common medication used is methylphenidate, sold under the brand name of Ritalin®. We will look at the action of these drugs in a later chapter.

As I mentioned earlier, the RAS seems to come into full maturity at around age 7. For this reason, many of the problems associated with the RAS - bed wetting, sleep walking, attention problems, tend to be outgrown at about this age.

NOTES

Chapter Three

The Central Nervous System-- Limbic System

If we journey a little further into the brain we will discover a complex region which accounts for our love of children, our frustration with children, our love of teaching as well as early teacher retirement. This region, referred to as the **limbic system,** is part of a larger region often called the **reptilian brain**. The name reflects the fact that it is the part of the brain we share with the reptilian class of animals.

Educators like to focus so much on the outer covering of the brain, the cortex, because we pride ourselves in developing that part of the brain. But what lies underneath may in fact play a stronger role in the learning process than we would like to believe. What evil lurks within this region? Let's take a look.

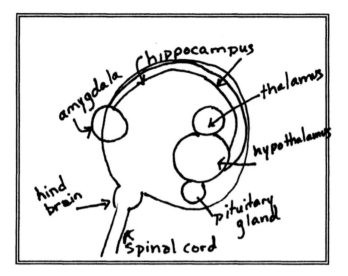

There are several subregions in this reptilian brain as illustrated in the drawing above. You will find the key players - the **thalamus**, the **hypothalamus**, the **amygdala**, the **pituitary gland** and the **hippocampus**.

The hippocampus may be an area you are somewhat familiar with as it is frequently in the media for its role in **Alzheimer's Disease**. The hippocampus forms new memories for us. In Alzheimer's disease, that region physically detaches and separates off from the rest of the region.

The Thalamus

An area you are probably less familiar with is the thalamus. The thalamus doesn't make it into the news very often and we don't encounter issues with it too much in the classroom, but it is a very nice area of the brain to have working properly.

The thalamus's job is to sort sensory data for us. All of our senses (except smell) send their input as raw data to the thalamus. The thalamus then must determine which sense it came from and send it to the correct part of the cortex to be interpreted.

For example, if I look at a flower, that image enters my eye as nerve impulses which are carried into my brain to be interpreted. The impulses go first to the thalamus which determines that the information was sent from my eyes, and it then forwards the information on to the visual cortex of my brain to be interpreted as the sight of a flower.

If my thalamus made a mistake, perhaps thought the information was sent from my ears, it would then send that data to the auditory center of the cortex where it would be interpreted as a sound. Now instead of seeing the flower, I would "hear" the flower. That is what is called a hallucination.

So hallucinations are not simply figments of your imagination, they are very real sensations that have been mis-interpreted. Most of us don't deal with these much in the classroom, unless we are working with children with severe emotional problems, like schizophrenia. These children often have some dysfunction in their thalamus which causes them to hallucinate. Or you may know or work with young people who think this is an interesting experience and use hallucinogenic drugs. Hallucinogenic drugs target the thalamus, thus the hallucinations.

Also, just for your own personal information, when the brain ages, this is one of the regions to deteriorate and so often times people will hallucinate in old age. I had a funny personal experience with this with my grandfather. I can easily remember my grandfather during the last year of his life. He told me about the people who came in through the ceiling of his bedroom every night to visit him. I asked him one day, "Grandpa, are these people that you know?"

His response, "Well, I didn't know them at first, but after they come a few nights we get to know each other pretty well." Where did the people come from in Grandpa's mind? Perhaps it was the feel of the bed sheets on his feet as he climbed into bed, or some other sensory stimuli that occurred each night. Often times the people coming and going in his house would frighten him because he never knew if they were real or imaginary, but then he learned to take his cue from his dog. If "Buddy" wasn't barking, they probably were not real and posed no threat.

The Hypothalamus

Located underneath the thalamus is the appropriately named, hypothalamus. This small region of the reptilian brain is enormous in terms of responsibility and behavior. The hypothalamus is considered to be the most primitive region of the brain that can drive a behavior. It comes in the brain at birth, fully functioning. It controls the so-called primitive emotions such as fear, anger, and aggression. It is also responsible for our fight-or-flight response, hunger, thirst, sex drive, body temperature, and water balance. It is also in charge of the endocrine system and thus ultimately controls all of our hormones. That's a lot of responsibility for one area.

The Hypothalamus Controls:
Fear
Anger
Aggression
Fight/flight response
Hunger
Thirst
Water Balance
Body Temperature
Hormones

The amygdala

Let's look further into the workings of the hypothalamus by examining its relationship with other regions of the reptilian brain. Move deeper to find the amygdala, a small almond-sized area responsible for some of our more sophisticated emotions, such as love, jealousy, attraction, kindness and compassion. The amygdala and the hypothalamus apparently stay in communication with each other via pathways along the hippocampus which not only relays information between those two, but also has an important job itself in forming new memories.

While the amygdala my be present in the brain at birth, a great deal of its function develops during childhood based on environmental cues, modeling and parenting. The amygdala is the second voice you hear in your head after someone has committed an injustice against you. If a student yells an obscenity at you, your first gut reaction ("kill"- or a variation on that theme) comes from your hypothalamus.

Let me give you an example of the development of this region. Think back to when you were a youngster of maybe five years. You got the new "Baby Thumbelina" for your birthday. She was your most treasured gift and you set her aside in your room, wrapped gently in a blanket to wait for you until after the birthday party. And you went back to your friends and the birthday party. In a little while, here comes your three year old brother. And he has your "Baby Thumbelina". And her clothes are missing. And she has Creepy Crawler goo running down her face and her feet are colored green. Now, what was your first, gut reaction? If you say, "Kill him," then you have heard the voice of the hypothalamus. The hypothalamus speaks first in everyone's head - its a very primitive region.

But your mother was fortunately standing nearby and kept you from actually killing your little brother as she recognized this wonderful amygdala-developing-moment. So Mom intervened with kind and gentle words like *"Oh, he's only three. He loves you so much. He didn't mean to hurt your doll. We can clean her up and she'll be good as new. Come on, give him a hug, let's have cake."*

Remember when Mom said things like that to you? If you are a lucky person, you have had lots of amygdala-developing-moments and that comes in real handy many years later when you are a classroom teacher and you have had what seems like your 30th run-in today with that "problem child."

We all hear first the voice of the hypothalamus that for a moment suggests that perhaps the world will be a better place with one less child in it. But the other parts of our brain are stronger and override that thought with kind and gentle words like *"You wanted to be a teacher because you love children. Kindness and patience are the best teachers. . .etc."*

Hopefully, if appropriate behavior other than aggression was modeled for you in your early years, the amygdala's voice is a strong one and will overrule the hypothalamus in most cases. We've all had this discussion in our heads, and being civilized people, reason and higher level emotions prevail and the child survives another day.

But most of us also know people who appear not to even own any of these overriding regions. They tend to only hear the voice of the hypothalamus and never the other voices. The hypothalamus is more primitive and when forced into a survival situation, we resort to the most primitive areas of our brain. Depending on upbringing and adult role models, the amygdala may or may not be a strong voice of reason which is listened to before action is taken. People who frequently exhibit this type of response are known as hypothalamus-driven individuals. Some days our classrooms seem to be full of them.

Research is shedding new light on what is referred to as a hypothalamus-driven individual. First of all, they do tend to be male. Sorry men, but the biggest biological brain difference between the genders seems to be the hypothalamus. In fact, that is generally the easiest way to sex a brain - look at the hypothalamus. The male hypothalamus is larger than the females. It's a product of testosterone and begins even prenatally. So, on the whole, men tend to drive more behaviors out of this region than women do.

The biggest reason however, for hypothalamus-driven behavior really is a result of the way in which the brain functions. Every time you think a thought, you fire a particular pathway in your brain. And every time you fire that pathway, it gets easy to fire. So the more often you think something, the easier it is to think.

Therefore, children who are raised in fight or flight worlds, tend to be hypothalamus-driven. Children who grow up in an environment where eat-or-be-eaten is the rule of the day, tend to function quite easily from their hypothalamus.

And finally, because children tend to learn how to handle an active hypothalamus by watching people in their world - children raised by hypothalamus-driven parents tend to be hypothalamus driven.

The good news to all of this is that it is never too late to develop the higher emotional portion of a child's brain. The easiest way to teach appropriate response to the hypothalamus, is through modeling the behavior yourself.

Whenever a parent or teacher is "caught" with their hypothalamus engaged with anger, it is a grand opportunity for teaching the young people who are standing nearby as observers.

Keep in mind that even for the most dysfunctional of children, operating in this state of mind is uncomfortable. The brain's desire is to get out of this state. The sad fact is that for many children, they do not know any other response. So often times a teacher's biggest responsibility is to model appropriate behavior when our own hypothalamus is engaged.

Students watch how we handle ourselves in tough situations. How do you handle a student who yells an obscenity? Do you react with your hypothalamus? Or do you wait until you calm down, engage higher areas of your brain and handle it with reason, understanding and a true desire to help the situation improve?

Let's go back to the earlier example of the problem child who has irritated you one more time today. Not only does the problem child know she has "pushed your button," the other students around her do too. All eyes are on you. The students are watching to see what your reaction will be. And what you do at that moment is what teaches conflict resolution - more so than all the conflict resolution curriculum you want to introduce this year. So what do you do at this moment?

The one thing you don't want to do is pretend that you are not angry. We do a big disservice to children when we try to invalidate the emotion of anger. It is not a childish emotion. It is a natural, healthy, adult human emotion. In fact, anger may be the best emotion we have as it is a fabulous energy source for change.

We have countless examples throughout history of this. The American Revolution probably would never have occurred if Sam Adams hadn't been angry. And Mothers Against Drunk Drivers (MADD) was begun from someone's anger. So you see, the problem children have is not with being angry - it's what they DO when they are angry that creates the problem.

What children (and some adults) need to understand is that when you are in the initial "kill him" frame of mind, there is not much activity in the brain north of the reptilian brain. In other words, because this whole system operates on a priority from the bottom, up, in a state of anger, the bulk of the brain's energy is concentrated no higher than this region.

This is not called the Reptilian Brain for nothing. We share it with the Reptilian class. So when you make a decision in this state of mind, you are thinking with all the wisdom of a turtle. For most of us, this is not our best mind. We need to wait. Wait for those higher thinking, reasoning areas of our brain to become engaged. How long do we need to wait? It depends (generally a lot longer than the proverbial "count to 10"). It varies due to a wealth of factors including how we are feeling today, what other things have happened to irritate us today, and the relationship we had with this individual before the situation even occurred. But wait is the key. Give yourself time to calm down, engage higher brain regions and make a better decision and response.

For a teacher, a comment as simple as *"Erika, I am so angry right now that I do not feel comfortable even discussing this. Can you please go sit right outside the door here until I calm down enough that I feel like I'm thinking more clearly"*. These are the sorts of things that children need to hear verbalized. Don't expect that they will catch all this simply hearing you sending Erika to the principal's office.

The bright side of the hypothalamus

I don't want to paint the hypothalamus with too dark of a color here, for there is a very sound and good biological reason for its power. We can see quite clearly why it is given such a big priority in the system and why that is a good thing. It ensures our survival.

There are three basic components to the survival of any creature. While many psychology books refer to these as the "3 F's of survival," I prefer Robert Sylwester's interpretation when he says that we make one of three decisions about everything we meet: we can EAT it, RUN from it, or MATE with it. And everything else is just a secondary issue.

You can see how your survival depends upon you making the correct decision. And all three of these behaviors are controlled by the hypothalamus. We can now see why it's given such a priority. It ensures our survival.

However, it only has a three word vocabulary, eat - kill-sex. That's all it knows. Well sometimes eat- kill- sex is a good thing because we'll live to see tomorrow. But sometimes, eat-kill-sex is not in our best long term interest. And THAT decision is made by the higher thinking parts of our brain.

The decision of whether or not this a good time for eat-kill-sex is made by the region I referred to earlier, the pre-frontal cortex. Located high up in the brain, in the sophisticated human region behind the forehead, the pre-frontal cortex is the voice of reason.

The pre-frontal cortex handles the big question - Is this a good time for eat-kill-sex or not? It brings in all sorts of reference material, analysis of past history, flow charts, T charts and probability factors and reasons its way to a decision. It then hands this decision down to the hypothalamus, by way of the amygdala who puts nice fuzzy emotions on it. The decision obviously comes in one of two forms, either *No*, this is not a good time for eat-kill-sex, or *Yes*, this looks like a good time for it. And sometimes the hypothalamus listens to that decision and sometimes it doesn't. Even in the brightest of people like you and I.

We have all heard the voice in our head that said , *"Ooohh, look at that cheesecake! Doesn't that look delicious. Let's have a large piece with the strawberry topping."* Then moments later you heard another voice in your head. This voice said *"Oh no, I don't think so! Do you know how many calories are in that cheesecake? Think of the fat grams. Do you know how long you'll have to run on your treadmill when you get home if you eat that cheesecake? You've done so good all week on your diet, let's not ruin it now with the cheesecake. NO cheesecake!"*

And 30 minutes later, the cheesecake is gone! And you have cheesecake on your hands. Oh the horror of it all! How can this happen?

You can now see where the voices come from. The voice that sounds, *"Eat cheesecake, big piece"* comes from the hypothalamus. The voice that reasons *"Eating the cheesecake is not in your best long term interest"* is from your pre-frontal cortex. On a good day that pre-frontal cortex wins out, but not always.

The Adolescent Brain

Those of us who parent, teach or own adolescents have often been frustrated with their behavior. The adolescent brain does in fact, operate very differently from the adult brain which sometimes causes tremendous frustration on both parts. The biggest difference in the adolescent brain comes in this relationship between the hypothalamus and the pre-frontal cortex.

The hypothalamus of an adolescent is very active. In fact much research supports the idea that the hypothalamus is at its highest level of activity during adolescence for several reasons.

First and foremost, the hormones associated with puberty and secondary sex characteristics tend to excite or increase activity in the hypothalamus. Secondly, adolescents are most influenced by their own peers and people tend to model hypothalamus behavior based on the people in their world. Since adolescents surround themselves with other adolescents you see them virtually swimming in a pool of hypothalamus behavior.

The other key factor in the adolescent brain is that the pre-frontal cortex takes about 21 years to fully mature. Prior to this time it functions, but not strongly and not without problems. So that sums up the adolescent brain. The voice that says "eat-kill-sex" is very loud, very strong, very constant. The voice that says "well, maybe not" is very distant and only works every other Tuesday. So those of us who work with adolescents often times need to be the voice of their pre-frontal cortex. Remember, just because the body is adult size, doesn't mean the brain housed within is an adult brain.

The Female Reptilian Brain

I don't want to be accused of having some type of gender bias against the male brain and its large hypothalamus, so let me finish this section with a note regarding a problem in this region with the female brain. The hypothalamus in some women is extremely sensitive to the excretions of another nearby region -the pituitary gland. It's a design problem really, resulting from the proximity of these two regions. The pituitary gland secretes, among other things, sex hormones. For men, that doesn't create too much of a problem because hormone levels remain relatively constant. (Yes, men do get a small increase in testosterone levels around 8:00 in the morning and a little bigger surge in the fall, but for the most part, they stay level).

For women, however, hormone levels are not constant. A women's brain can be walking along fine one day, minding its own business, when suddenly - squirt! - here comes a bunch of *leutinizing hormone* from the pituitary, gushing all over the hypothalamus. You may just be recovering from this shock, when- squirt! - here comes a bunch of *follicle stimulating hormone*, gushing out all over the hypothalamus.

Now some women have a hypothalamus that doesn't like that. In fact they are particularly sensitive to this erratic and unannounced hormone activity. If you go back and look again at the responsibilities of the hypothalamus- anger, aggression, eating, thirst, sex drive, water balance, body temperature - you may begin to see a correlation here. This is an event affectionately known as pre-menstrual syndrome, or PMS. The next time someone says it is all in your head, you can agree, "yes, it certainly is."

Chapter Four

Classroom Management

Because of the emotional aspect of classroom management, it always seems fitting to bring up a discussion on it when we are looking at this middle, emotional part of the brain.

From a practical standpoint, one of the easiest ways to engage the hypothalamus of anyone is to take away their perception of control. When people are backed into a corner and feel that they are powerless or have no control whatsoever over their situation, the hypothalamus becomes engaged. Once that happens we see destructive, angry, and aggressive behaviors. In a classroom, this means teachers that teach in a *"my way or no way"* manner.

If I present myself as the ultimate dictator and controller of the environment, the rules, the curriculum and the learning styles in my domain, then it should not come as a surprise to see destructive behavior or angry, defiant and aggressive behaviors at times. Although the students may in fact be quite "disciplined" in my presence, the emotions that are evoked here are particularly damaging to the learning process.

Students need to feel that they have some input somewhere, either in helping decide classroom policies, assignment choices, or both. In just about any course, any curriculum, and any teaching style, there is room for input of some sort, no matter how small, from students. Allowing students to feel that they have some control over their situation will create a huge decrease in classroom management problems. And it is one of the easiest things teachers can do.

Some students have a very strong hypothalamus. Many because they are raised in an environment where fight-or-flight is the daily norm. Many because the only adults in their life are also driven by their hypothalamus. One of our most important jobs as teacher and parent is as a role model. We must model appropriate alternative behavior. Remember, you may be the only adult in their life that can react to situations with a brain part other than the hypothalamus. Ideally, you want to react after logical alternatives have been examined in the highest region of our brain - the cortex.

Classroom management styles

Teachers and parents also need to be wary of the way in which they use punishment as a management devise. Let's examine some of the basics of classroom management and parenting. You may remember from some educational psychology class you had long ago, that classroom management revolves around one of two concepts - **reinforcement** and **punishment**. Regardless of what type of classroom management you subscribe to, they all center on these two concepts.

Reinforcement - Any consequence to a behavior that increases the likelihood of that behavior occurring again.

Punishment - Any consequence to a behavior that decreases the likelihood of that behavior occurring again.

To review, reinforcement is any strategy or consequence designed to strengthen a behavior or increase the chance of it occurring again (hence the root: reinforce). Punishment on the other hand is a strategy or consequence designed to weaken a behavior or decrease the chances of the behavior occurring again.

Both of these come in positive and negative varieties, which frequently leads to some confusion. The confusion stems from our association with the word "positive" as meaning something good, while "negative" generally means something bad. You can forget those uses in this situation.

The terms come from archaic psychology data using the symbols '+' and '-' or plus and minus. Think in math terms, not good and bad. Positive means plus, or adding something, and Negative means minus or taking something away. In a moment we will see why the confusion has caused a great deal of misunderstanding in behavior management.

positive (+) to add something	negative (-) to take away something
reinforcement strengthen behavior	**reinforcement** strengthen behavior
punishment weaken behavior	**punishment** weaken behavior

You can see from the table above that if I want to strengthen a behavior I can do that by either adding to the situation or taking something away (positive or negative reinforcement).

Let me use an example. If my son came home with straight A's on his report card - definitely a behavior I'd like to see happen again, I could reinforcement him by adding something to his life - his favorite dinner, a trip to the mall for the new shoes he's been wanting, use of my car, etc. Interestingly, money, one of the most common positive reinforcers parents use, is inappropriate here for a variety of reasons, but is still a positive reinforcer.

I can also reinforce the behavior by taking something away - negative reinforcers. We must be careful here - this is where people get confused. If my son came home with straight A's, what can I take away from him that would strengthen the behavior? How about his chores, his obligation to clean up after dinner tonight, his curfew on Friday.

While these negative reinforcers are hard to think up, they are in fact, the strongest teaching- learning devise known to man. In reality, people will do ANYTHING, if you will take away something unpleasant. There is nothing stronger than a negative reinforcer.

If when I asked a moment ago to list things I could take away from my son, your first thoughts were things like his car, his computer, his phone, you have made one of the most common errors in all of psychology. Let me state this clearly: NEGATIVE REINFORCERS ARE NOT PUNISHMENT.   You can see why people get them confused. Negative sounds like something bad, so we think they are punishment - they are NOT. They are reinforcers. They STRENGTHEN behavior. This can be very good(if you are reinforcing a positive behavior).

Now, let's look at punishment. It too comes in both positive (add) and negative (take away) varieties. For an example, suppose my son came home breaking curfew for the second week in a row - a behavior I would definitely like to decrease or do away with. I may choose to use a positive or negative punishment for that. A positive punishment would be adding something to his life like additional chores, adding more time to his curfew, etc. I can also use a negative punishment and subtract things from his life, like the phone, the car, his computer, his allowance, etc.

I hope you can now see how distinctly different these four treatments are: positive reinforcement, negative reinforcement, positive punishment and negative punishment. I hope you can now see how very different negative reinforcement is from punishment, though the terms are used interchangeably at an alarming frequency even by professionals who should know better.

Once this is all clear, then let me shift your thinking a bit by also mentioning what psychologists and researchers have known for as long as they've studied human behavior - as a learning/teaching devise, punishment does not work. Punishment is ineffective, rather damaging and basically a useless technique. With that in mind, one wonders why the heck it is so popular. In fact it is pervasive in our society! It is the number one way we raise our children, it is the number one way we run our schools, and it is the number one way we run our society. And yet it doesn't work.

Why is it so popular? Your gut response to that question may be "because it's easy." A very common response, but a very wrong one too. Punishment is not easy. In fact, it is a very difficult way to handle learning.

Let me use another example to help illustrate the point. Imagine you and a group of your colleagues each have a small puppy. Your job is to teach the puppy to sit at the voice command, "sit" and you have an hour to get the job done. Just to add a little incentive I may offer you $10,000 if you can succeed.

Do you have a plan? I'll bet your plan does not involve a rolled up newspaper. But maybe your colleague Frank uses that plan. In fact Frank runs to his car to get today's newspaper, rolls it up, says to the puppy "Sit!" and when the puppy fails to comply, Frank swats her with the newspaper. Wow - can you believe Frank would do that? Just when you were beginning to think Frank was such a bright individual he goes and does something so stupid. That's what you are thinking, isn't it?

In fact, I imagine 99% of your colleagues will be thinking of a plan similar to your plan which goes something like:

> *"perhaps I can go get yesterday's leftover donuts out of my car - dogs like donuts. Then I'll say to the puppy "sit" and press his little puppy bottom down while smiling and saying "oh, good puppy, good puppy, here have a donut."*

You see, the reality of the situation, which everyone (except Frank) seems to know almost intuitively is, **if your goal is truly to change behavior, we would never use punishment**. We all know that. We all do that. The problem with punishment is that when we use it, our goal is not to change behavior, it is to get ourselves out of a hypothalamus state of mind.

Yes, the act of punishing is negatively reinforcing to the person doing the punishing and that is the number one reason it persists in popularity in our society.

To go back to the earlier example of my son coming home breaking curfew for the second week in a row - what if as I confront him, he rolls his eyes, shrugs his shoulders, heads to his room and turns the music up to full volume behind a closed door. Can you feel my pain? Can you see which part of my brain is now glowing red? Yes, the old hypothalamus has raised its ugly head in Mom. And as everyone knows, if Mom's not happy, nobody is happy.

As mentioned earlier, this is not a pleasant state of mind. It is uncomfortable. I want out of this mind set and quickly. The quickest way out of this state is to inflict some type of pain on the object of my anger - in this case my son. I can inflict physical pain, emotional pain, social pain, anything will do. The very act of punishing him will make me feel so much better. Unfortunately though, the person in this situation who has learned something valuable is me. I've learned that the next time I'm in an uncomfortable, angry state of mind, the quickest way to relieve that discomfort is to punish.

My son, on the other hand has learned some not so good things. He has learned all the same things that your colleague Frank's puppy learned. Remember Frank and the puppy he was hitting with the newspaper? Can you picture what that puppy is learning as she's being hit with the newspaper? Her body language is probably saying fear. If she's not tied up, she's probably going to run out of the room about the third time Frank comes at her with the paper. And if she is tied up, she's probably going to try to snap at Frank after a few swats with the newspaper. The sad thing here is that punishment DOES teach. It teaches fear, aggression and avoidance and in very unpredictable amounts.

Punishment teaches :
- fear
- aggression
- avoidance

My son doesn't learn that next time he wants to come home on time. He learns next time don't get caught. Next time come home quieter. Next time don't come home at all. Punishment results in these emotions which by the way, all stem from the hypothalamus. So even more dangerous is the fact that punishment based schemes directly strengthen and reinforce the very hypothalamus behaviors we are trying to reduce.

This is a very disturbing concept for most of us as parents and teachers. We were raised on punishment, we were taught punishment based schemes in teacher education courses. They all seem so popular and so right. Besides, it's not like we should just let kids get away with bad behavior, right?

True enough. There is no magic solution here, but I want to caution you to their overuse and to the mistaken belief that somehow the child is benefitting from the act of punishment. We are humans, we have feelings, emotions and we have the right to act out on them sometimes. Even my own personal four children sometimes just catch me on a bad day and they may experience my wrath. But I am fully aware at the moment that this is doing very little for the child, though I really don't care because we're dealing with my issues right now and we can deal with their issues tomorrow.

It may make you feel a little better to know that from a practical standpoint we cannot and even do not want to do completely away with punishment based strategies in parenting and in teaching. They do serve a very useful purpose. First of all, it would be tough to get rid of punishment completely in our classrooms because that would mean that we had the following philosophy:

> *Here are the classroom/school rules & policies. He or she who follows them, gets to stay.*

Can you see an immediate problem with this idea? *Getting to stay* needs to be a good thing. And for many of our students they just don't see it that way. In fact, getting to leave may seem like the reward. So often times we have to force them into a situation they don't find enjoyable.

The other reason for punishment in schools and homes is that really, you do need a little bit of fear in your relationship with your children. This is because with fear, you get blind obedience to authority. And sometimes you need that. If my youngest son is running out in front of an approaching vehicle this is not a time for us to discuss creative alternate strategies. In fact, quite the opposite. I need to be able to shout "stop" and he will - no questions asked. That is blind obedience to authority and you get it through fear.

If I am in charge of a classroom full of children, and I for some reason need to take absolute and immediate control, I need to be able to do that. You get that obedience with fear. So for that reason, a little bit of punishment is not a bad thing. But punishment comes with a cost. It costs you creativity, problem solving and higher level thinking.

So while punishment will give you nice obedient children, it won't give you creative, thinking children. It's a balancing act for us as teachers and parents. You need to use enough punishment to give you the control you must have, but not so much as to stifle all creative thinking.

NOTES

Chapter Five

Substance Use and Abuse in the Lower and Reptilian Brain

Although drug use involves many areas of the brain, the reptilian brain, or limbic system is a good region to start the discussion as so many recreational drugs have their main effect here, specifically in the amygdala.

If you take the neurotransmitter dopamine and inject it into your amygdala, it feels really good. (For additional information on the amygdala, see chapter three). Go ahead, try it. To do so, just wander into your favorite fantasy. Imagine your happy place. Perhaps it is lying on the beach in a tropical paradise, scuba diving for buried treasure, or simply a quiet romantic evening with your favorite film star. When you visit that happy place it should feel good. You will know you are successful if there is a smile on your face.

What you physically are doing is secreting dopamine into your amygdala. Amazing, isn't it, that we can change the neurochemistry in our brains just through a simple cognitive exercise. You can do this pretty much as often as you like or as often as you can get away with.

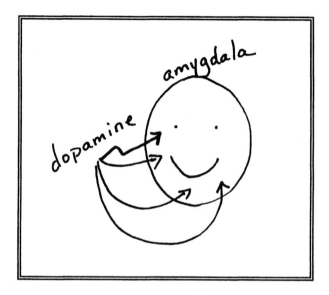

It should come as no surprise that humans long ago wondered if perhaps they could come up with something artificial, that could be ingested at will, which would secrete a whole bunch of dopamine into the amygdala to give us a pleasurable sensation greater than we could manage with our own fantasy thoughts.

And being the cleaver creatures that we are, it didn't take long to come up with these things. They are called recreational drugs. The two biggest ones that work this way are alcohol and crack cocaine.

Alcohol has many actions on the brain and body, but the action that is associated with the pleasure experience of that drug is that it secretes large amounts of dopamine into the amygdala. Now that doesn't sound like such a bad idea. And it wouldn't be if not for the body's need for homeostasis. Homeostasis remember, is the body's drive and determination to keep everything the same. Or at least close to it.

In chapter one we looked at homeostasis in the body's response to caffeine, Caffeine mimics a natural neurotransmitter and its regular use causes the body to reduce its own production in order to maintain ideal levels. This then is the same problem encountered with alcohol use as well as several other types of recreational drugs.

Alcohol causes large amounts of dopamine to be injected into the amygdala. It feels good, but the brain, like the rest of the body doesn't like anyone playing with neurotransmitter levels. So after a little while the brain tries to compensate for this by reducing its own dopamine production.

This is stage one of addiction: the reduction of dopamine production. In layman's terms we refer to this as drug tolerance. So if you notice that back in college you could get a nice warm glow off of a glass of wine, but today you need the entire bottle, then you know tolerance. What's happened is your body has reduced its own production of dopamine and now you need more of the drug to give you the same effect.

Well, for many people, that's not a problem. They simply increase their consumption of the drug. Now the brain moves into stage two: reducing and removing dopamine receptor sites. Receptor sites are those points on the amygdala where the dopamine attaches. If there are no receptor sites, the dopamine cannot attach and cannot trigger a response from the amygdala.

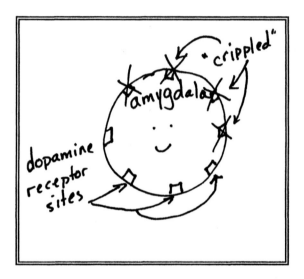

This stage two process will continue until all, or nearly all of the receptor sites are removed or shut down. Now the individual has what the literature refers to as the **crippled brain.**

You can see the problem for the alcoholic or cocaine addict who wants to quit. They no longer want to be addicted to alcohol or cocaine. How does this person then experience pleasure? They don't. The whole system has been crippled to the point where they cannot experience pleasure, they can only come close to feeling even normal emotions through huge amounts of the drug that will trigger the last few receptor sites remaining on the amygdala.

It is easy to see why recovery is so difficult. We can see why depression is so great and suicide rate so high among recovering addicts. If left alone, sometimes these receptor sites will rebuild and sometimes they don't. Apparently you can permanently cripple this system though substance abuse.

The rate at which the brain moves through this process varies widely. Some brains move quickly, some more slowly. The speed at which the brain adjusts tends to be the part of addiction that is genetic. Some of us are lucky enough to have the not so clever brains and can tolerate a moderate amount of substance use. Others of us have inherited the clever brains that adjust to changing conditions rather quickly. These are the brains prone to addiction problems.

Here again is another opportunity for those of us who work and live with adolescents. They need to be aware of the risk they take when experimenting with substance use. While it may be fine for some, it is disastrous for others.

Adolescent brains, in general do not tolerate alcohol use. Because one of the other key areas that alcohol affects is the pre frontal cortex, adolescents are advised to refrain from its use until the age of 21 or 22 when that area has matured. Alcohol is very damaging to the developing pre-frontal cortex. The adult brain tends to be able to tolerate moderate amounts. The adolescent brain cannot.

Another drug, gaining popularity at an alarming rate is the drug **Ecstasy**. As of this writing, Ecstasy use has spread to about 12% of the nation's high school population - quite a statistic given the newness of the drug. It caught on very quickly primarily under the guise of being a relatively "safe" drug.

Nothing could be further from the truth. Ecstasy not only plays around with dopamine levels in the brain, it affects serotonin levels as well. Ecstasy use is associated with long term memory problems, obsessive-compulsive disorder, depression and a host of other mental distresses.

This same scenario of brain adjustment comes into play with pharmaceutical treatments as well. As most of us know, the pharmaceutical industry has exploded over the last several decades in terms of treatments for mental disorders. Despite the negative publicity often given these treatments, the fact remains that only a tiny fraction of people are housed in mental institutions today compared with the middle of the last century. And nearly all of that reduction is due primarily to advancements in the pharmaceutical industry for mental illness treatments. No one can question the improvements they have made in the quality of many lives let alone the saving of lives.

One of the first big areas that drug companies "dappled in" if you will, is depression. The chemistry of clinical depression has been known for quite a long time. The culprit is serotonin. Serotonin is another brain neurotransmitter responsible for a huge number of functions and behaviors. But if you have low levels of it in certain parts of your brain, then you have depression. Women tend to have lower amounts naturally compared to men, which is why we tend to be more prone to depression.

Anyway, back to our story about the drug companies. They knew years ago that if your serotonin levels got too low in some brain regions, you became depressed. So it only made sense that the first attempt at treating depression was with artificial serotonin. And in fact, that's what they did. They put artificial serotonin in a tablet and gave it to persons with depression. Lo and behold - it worked. For awhile.

Sure enough artificial serotonin will remove depression, but you can see that your time will be limited here as eventually the brain will make the same adjustments for the varied serotonin levels as it does for any other type of artificial neurotransmitter. So after awhile, the brain started cutting back on its own serotonin production which led to some very serious side effects.

So, the drug companies realized they needed to try a different approach. Today they treat depression and a host of other illnesses by taking advantage of something called a **re-uptake mechanism**. To understand the way this works, we need to go back to our original drawing of a neuron and its communication with other neurons.

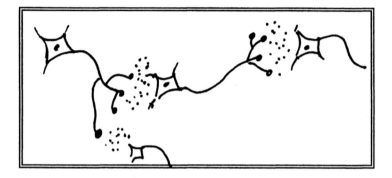

Remember that when one neuron or nerve cell needs to communicate with another cell it does so by releasing chemicals into the synapse between the cells. The chemicals (neurotransmitters such as serotonin or dopamine) then flood across the space and trigger the neighboring cell to fire. When their work is finished, the neurotransmitters are not discarded - that would be wasteful. The body is a wonderful recycling devise.

When neurotransmitters are finished in the synapse, the cell uses a tiny vacuum cleaner type attachment to slurp the chemicals back out of the synapse to be recycled into the cell. This vacuum cleaners are called re-uptake mechanisms.

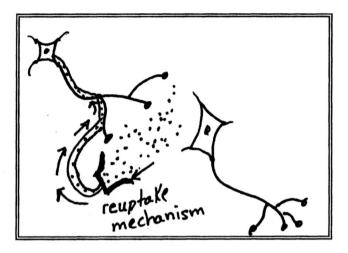

reuptake mechanism

Most doctors today treat depression with something called a serotonin re-uptake inhibitor. Their name is rather self-explanatory. The drugs work not by providing an artificial serotonin, but rather by shutting down the vacuum cleaner attachments on the neurons. This allows the person's body to make its own natural amount of serotonin, but shuts off the re-uptake so it stays out in the synapse for a longer period of time and gives the impression of additional serotonin levels. This appears to be a much more effective treatment over the long term.

The earliest drug which worked this way was sold under the name of Prozac®. Today they use even more sophisticated drugs such as Paxil® and Zoloft® which mixes a serotonin re-uptake inhibitor with a norepinephrine re-uptake inhibitor. Many of the pharmaceuticals used today work by inhibiting the re-uptake of one or more neurotransmitters.

Drug companies have found other ways to increase neurotransmitter levels without using mimics including monoamine oxidase inhibitors (MAO) which work by shutting down enzymes that destroy specific neurotransmitters. The next chapter will also explain neurotrophins which are now being used as another treatment for depression. But the majority of the treatments we see students receiving work by inhibiting the re-uptake mechanisms.

This is also the principle behind treating attention deficit disorder. You can get some improvement in ADD with caffeine use. A little caffeine generally will reduce the impulsivity seen with ADD. The problem with using this as a treatment, as you can probably already see, is that you would have to constantly keep increasing the amounts as the body would start to compensate for the changing levels. So most people who look to pharmaceuticals for ADD, will use something like methylphenidate sold under the name Ritalin®.

This drug is a dopamine re-uptake inhibitor. It works by slowing down the re-uptake mechanisms for dopamine. Since attention deficit disorder tends to be caused by problems with dopamine levels, it turns out to be a fairly good treatment. There is actually some research to support the idea that the best treatment for ADD/HD is actually Ritalin® mixed with caffeine!

Some of the newer treatments for ADD are using more of the cocktail approach seen with depression - they are mixing dopamine re-uptake inhibitors with other neurotransmitter re-uptake inhibitors because not all brains are equal and some people have different neurotransmitter imbalances than others.

Ritalin® is a registered trademark of Novartis Pharmaceuticals Corp.

Paxil® is a registered trademark of Glaxo SmithKline.

Zoloft® is a registered trademark of Pfizer, Inc.

NOTES

Chapter Six

The Cerebral Cortex

At last, after many chapters, we've reached the top in our journey through the brain. We can see why education is such a difficult task. This whole system works on a priority from the bottom, up. And we are trying to teach to the top. It is amazing that we ever get there. But get there we do and at the top we find the **cerebral cortex**. The cortex is the wrinkled outer shell to the brain and the part most of us think of when we think of the brain.

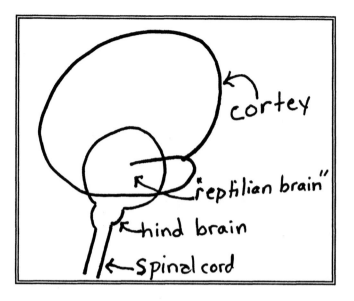

Humans are so proud of our cortex - and rightly so. It can do so much. It is the site of all of our formal learning. Here is where we store our knowledge, history, math, music, science, geography, language, reasoning skills, and even our ability to do crossword puzzles and write poetry. It is the source of our creativity, our humor, our ability to problem solve.

And all this is done on a sheet of tissue only six cell layers thick and about the thickness of a quarter! The cortex of the brain is only six cells deep. It is laid out in a thin rectangular sheet of tissue comprised mostly of nerve cells stacked in column of six. It coils and wraps itself around the reptilian brain so it appears to be a thick and wrinkled mass sitting on the top of our brain.

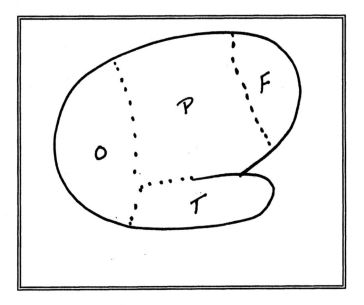

The cortex is divided into 4 main lobes or regions, each responsible for some broad categories of thinking. The back lobe is the **occipital lobe** and is primarily responsible for vision. It stores, interprets and works with visual information. The parts over the ears are called the **temporal lobes** and they are primarily concerned with hearing and understanding and producing verbal language. The top part is the **parietal lobe** and it handles most of the body's incoming sensory information. Finally, the front of the brain, right behind our forehead, is called the **frontal lobe**. It is unique to humans and apparently is what separates us from all the other animals. It is our decision maker. It is also involved in speech and anticipating new situations, problem solving and some memories.

Lobes of the Cortex:
- occipital
- parietal
- temporal
- frontal

Although the lobes are generally shown as separate regions, rarely does one region or lobe of the brain respond or fire in isolation. Most thoughts, creative products and learning activities involve communication between many areas of the brain. They communicate by firing electrical/chemical signals along neurons to create what are called neural pathways.

For example, let's look at the simple act of eating a warm slice of homemade bread. You will see the bread using nerve cells in your visual area. That image is paired with previous memories you may have of bread, including other situations, good and bad that you associate with bread. This experience could elicit an emotional response as well which will be handled in a different region below the cortex. You may smell the bread and even anticipate the taste by salivating in your mouth. You coordinate enough motor skills to bring it to your mouth and take a bite. If the bread has a peculiar or unique flavor today, you may add this new memory, via the hippocampus to previously stored categories of memories involving similar experiences. There were many neural pathways fired during this eating experience.

Every moment of every day you fire pathways of neurons through the cortex of your brain. Every time you fire a particular pathway it gets easier to fire. The next chapter looks at how we build these pathways through life's experiences to shape the brain we bring into adulthood.

This shaping process, while intense in childhood continues throughout our life. It is a process without end.

NOTES

Chapter Seven

Neuron Development in the Cortex

We will now examine neural pathway firings in greater detail. Remember the lonely neuron from chapter one? It resides in your brain surrounded by billions of others. In fact, you are born with approximately 200 billion neurons in your brain. One might think that we have close to that same number today, or even more. But actually we have about half that number.

During the first ten or twelve years of life we manage to whittle the number of neurons in our brain from 200 billion to 100 billion. In fact the demise of neurons in large numbers begins even before birth. Estimates are that the number of nerve cells peaks at around 525 billion neurons around 26 weeks gestation. It's a bit disturbing to think that we are born with half our brains already gone and it's been heading downhill ever since!

Obviously intelligence must be more complicated than shear numbers of neurons or we're all in trouble. Indeed, learning, knowledge and brain efficiency is not based on neuron numbers, but on dendrite numbers. **Dendrites**, are the branches on the neuron. You cannot grow new neurons in your brain (yes, some new research is shedding doubt on that in the hippocampus, but we'll cover that in the next edition) but you can grow new neuron branches.

You can grow these branches all the days of your life - and you should. This is the physical response in the brain to learning. Every time you learn something new you grow new connections or dendrites between nerve cells.

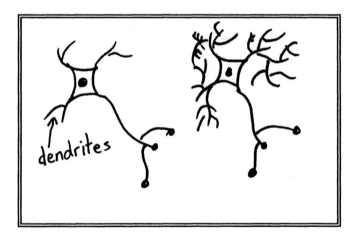

Each time you learn something new, each time you have a new experience, or are exposed to some sort of stimuli, new branches are literally grown on your neurons in order for them to communicate to other neurons and "pathways" are established. Young brains grow these branches very rapidly. We see the peak of dendrite development between our second and third birthday. Young children in exciting environments can grow these branches at the rate of 30,000 per second. That's an incredible amount of branching. Dendrites and neurons which are never used or are used very infrequently are pruned out to make way for new branches and stronger pathways through the brain. In fact each time you fire a particular pathway in your brain, it becomes easier to fire.

Let's use two examples to examine how pathways may fire through a visual input. Here is your brain on your birthday, brand new, with 200 billion neurons ready for action.

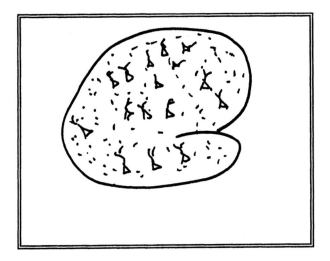

What was the first thing you saw? Perhaps the doctor's face. Let's suppose it fired a pathway of neurons through your brain like this:

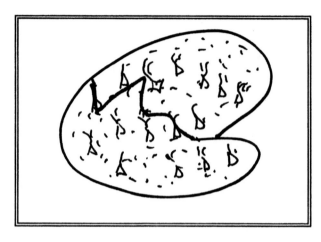

Keep in mind, the more often you fire a pathway, the stronger it becomes, and the easier it is to fire in the future. That said, how many times have you fired that particular pathway? If you're like me, you have never seen that doctor's face again. So what's happened to that pathway? It has most likely faded off into the sunset and was removed years ago. Let's try a different path.

What might have been the second thing you saw? Maybe your mother's face. Let's suppose the sight of your mother's face fired a pathway of neurons through your brain like this:

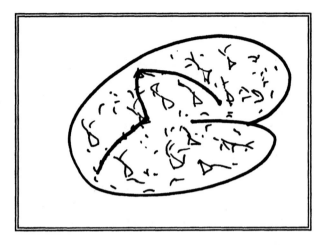

Now how many times have you seen your mother's face since then? I hope more than the doctor's. You have probably seen it thousands of times. So that pathway has been fired thousands of times and is quite strong and easy to fire.

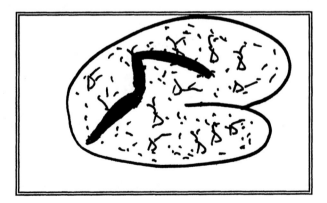

For this reason, the sight of your mother should cause instant recognition for you. You should not have the sensation of looking at her and getting a vague feeling of having seen her somewhere before, but can't quite place it.

So pathways fire, neurons grow new dendrites or branches on the tree and old branches and neurons are physically removed to make room for more elaborate and well established branches.

Think of this process as basic gardening. Everyone who gardens knows that you don't keep everything that sprouts up out of the ground. You prune and space seedling out to make room for bigger, healthier plants. Where I live Morning Glories grow as weeds in our gardens and are a constant problem as they spread out and choke off all the other weaker plants in their path. That's how your neurons grow. Well used neurons are strong and grow many, many branches to help connect one neuron to another or even to create micro-circuits within the same cell.   Smaller, less used ones that are in the way are simply removed.

Neuron Decay

The neuron removal process is indeed a relatively simple process. If a nerve cell is used regularly, it keeps a steady flow of blood passing by to drop off food and oxygen and haul away waste - that's true with all body cells.   But what happens when a cell in not used regularly? When that happens, there is a decrease in the demand for blood flow. After all, if you're not working, you don't need food delivery or garbage pick-up service. So now circulation in that area declines and the little bit of garbage produced by the cell starts to accumulate and build up. The garbage here that plays a significant role is calcium ions.

Calcium ions are the "garbage" of nerve cells. If blood doesn't flow by once in a while to pick up the garbage it just starts piling up and piling up around the cell. When the calcium ion levels reach a significant level it triggers the release of an enzyme inside the cell called **Calpain**. Calpain causes **autolysis** or the destruction of the neuron. It's a suicide bomber for lack of a better term - for the cell. When this enzyme is secreted, the cell literally blows up.

So that's how the brain gets rid of unused or little-used nerve cells. If they are not used, blood flow decreases to them. When blood flow decreases, the calcium ions tend to build up around the cell. At a certain calcium ion level, calpain is released by the cell and the cell is destroyed. A very simple process, really.

Neuron Growth and Maintenance

New growth, on the other hand, comes in the dendrite development, or branching of well-used neurons. This branching is caused from chemicals known as **Neurotrophins.** Neurotrophins are a group of proteins which are responsible for the growth and development of neurons. As you may suspect, we use a lot of neurotrophins during childhood as the brain has massive growth and development. But we continue to use neurotrophins all of our lives, especially in the hippocampus area, the brain region responsible for new learning and new memory formation.

There are many neurotrophins at work in the brain. The first one discovered is known as NGF (nerve growth factor). Others, discovered since, have equally self-explanatory names as BDNF (brain derived neurotrophic factor) and GDNF (glial cell-line derived neurotrophic factor). These neurotrophins work by attaching themselves to receptor sites on nerve cells and causing the cell membrane to change shape, grow and branch. Different neurotrophins work in different column levels of the cortex.

Most common known neurotrophins:

> **NGF**- nerve growth factor
> **BDNF** - brain-derived neurotrophic factor
> **NT-3** - neurotrophin-3
> **NT- 4/5** neurotrophin - 4/5
> **GDNF** - glial cell-line derived neurotrophic factor

There is some new research now which supports the idea that neurotrophins may also be partly responsible for the death of some cells as well - especially early death.
Researcher Barbara Hempstead at Cornell University has been the leader in this new research. Her team has discovered that as the neurotrophins themselves begin to form, some of them detach from the protein factory a

bit early. These immature chemicals, called **proneurotrophins** can actually end up binding to cells in their immature state and lead to the death of that cell. This has opened up a whole new area of research on Alzheimer's disease which is thought to be linked to this activity.

Developing neural pathways

A single neuron may be involved in many different pathways. So strengthening a neuron used for one project may have additional benefits if it is also used for other tasks.

A good example of this is seen in the math-music relationship in the brain. Years ago researchers discovered that children who were exposed to music at an early age tend to do better in math. The reason for this is that math and music use essentially the same brain region and the window of opportunity for working on this area is between birth and four years of age. So children who were exposed to music during this time period grew very well branched neurons. Children who were not exposed to music at this early age, did not.

If years later, these are the neurons we will use in a math class, you can easily see that the child with the more branched neurons will have an easier time handling math than the child with the pitiful branched(or what I refer to as "Charlie Brown Christmas Tree) neurons.

So although the branching took place at a young age and through music, the first brain had an advantage in math because these same neurons were already well developed with strong numerous branches.

Another area where we are beginning to see an advantage to well branched neurons is in Alzheimer's disease. The current research is strengthening the theory that people with more developed (more branched) neurons will be less affected by Alzheimer's disease than those without well developed branches.

In general, life is easier for the person with the most branches. And this is critical information for our students to understand. Just about every teacher has been asked at least once by a student, "*why are we having to learn this stuff? when are we ever going to use it?*"

Students often think that school is just preparing them for some giant Trivial Pursuit game later in life. They think they are supposed to be soaking up all this information because you never know when someone may walk up to you and ask: "*Pardon me, but can you tell me the bio-chemical byproducts of the Krebs cycle?*"

We are not asking children to learn all this material so that they can play Trivial Pursuit. Sure, some things are essential for day to day living and increase the quality of life, but the majority of what is taught is probably never going to have to be retrieved.

Instead, we are asking them to learn new material simply to help grow dendrites. We want to help them develop strong neural pathways in their brains so that their brain is useful to them all their life. Remind them, once you grow a branch you can keep that branch all your life and use it for more interesting endeavors.

I like to compare it to weight lifting. If you lift weights regularly, no one thinks the purpose of the activity is to one day be able to lift the weight upon request. The purpose is to develop a muscle that can someday be used for a different purpose. The same holds true for the brain. It is a 'use-it-or-lose-it' organ. If you use it, the neurons grow strong and well branched and you will have a quite useful brain you can use all your life. If you don't use it, the branches and cells wither away and are pruned out.

The easiest time to grow these branches seems to be between birth and 19 years of age. After that the chemistry changes in the brain and the branching becomes much more difficult. Students need to understand that the neurons they are born with are what I call "Charlie Brown Christmas Tree" neurons. It is up to them to grow them into mighty oaks.

"Charlie Brown Christmas Tree" neuron

"The Mighty Oak" neuron

Chapter Eight

The How and When of Growing Dendrites

Because most growth hormones throughout the body are especially active during sleep, it is thought that the majority of neurotrophic work is also done during sleep. In other words the actual branching of the nerve cells occurs primarily at night during sleep or more specifically, during various times of our sleep cycle.

You may have seen pictures of sleep cycles before. They are quite simple. You fall asleep near the top of the picture, fall into deeper and deeper sleep until you hit the bottom of the cycle, called delta sleep. Then you start climbing back up out of the cycle and enter your first period of **REM**.

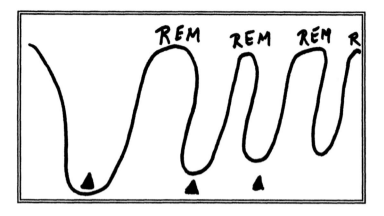

REM stands for rapid eye movement and is a period of intense dreaming activity. After about 10 minutes of dreaming you start back into the sleep cycle again. Each cycle takes about 90 minutes and you usually go through about 4 or 5 of these non-REM/ REM periods per good night's sleep

The work of Marcos Frank and Michael Stryker, at UC San Francisco, caught the neuropsychology and education worlds by surprise in 2001 with their startling research showing the tremendous amount of branching and subsequent learning that took place during the sleep cycle.

And what was a further surprise was that the bulk of the activity takes places during the non-REM cycles of sleep.. While most of the science community historically considered that the REM, or dreaming cycle of sleep was the time when most wiring took place, Stryker's work and the research following that study continue to show that it is actually the non-REM cycles that help hard wire in the information learned the previous day.

In fact, the research showed that if you study material and then sleep on it, you actually grow twice the number of neural connections as an individual who studies the material but doesn't sleep afterward.

> Sleeping after learning grows **twice** as many neural dendrites as learning the material did.

Much research has followed Stryker's study and continues to be one of the "hot" research areas today. And the research continues to support the idea that the bulk of learning takes place during sleep - or at least the hard wiring. There appears to be a window of time during which a student must wire in the previous days learning, or it will never be wired in.

Children who are sleep deprived after learning new information are unable to process and use that information as well as children who are not sleep deprived. The growing body of research says we as parents and educators have grossly underestimated the importance of sleep to the learning process. The idea that they can catch up on Saturday no longer holds.

If you work with adolescents, you know that due to their unique biological clocks, they tend to want to stay up later than most adults who run on a different biological clock. This doesn't mesh with the fact that adolescents still need to wake up at least as early as adults, in order to get to school on time. Most adolescents do not get their necessary requirement of sleep.

With all the research emerging on sleep, educators, parents, and school boards are becoming increasingly concerned about students' sleep habits. Because we now see that sleep not only is a time for cells and general body tissues to heal, refresh, and repair, it is also the time when our brain maintenance is in full swing. Sleep is the time when nerve cells branch in our brains, hardwiring in the day's learning. As a teacher and parent this is a serious concern.

So just how much sleep is enough sleep? While individual bodies vary, there are some general rules of thumb for sleep. We've heard for years that we need 8 hours of sleep at night, but the truth is that the length varies widely and the amount tends to decrease with age.

Young children need tremendous amounts of sleep not only because they are growing, but because their brains require a great deal of maintenance time.

So how much is enough? What you really should be doing is going to bed at night and sleeping until your body says, *"OK, we're done here, wake up."* Unfortunately most of us override the body's own system with such things as alarm clocks, thereby depriving ourselves of a properly maintained brain.

The average adult needs 7 hours of sleep a night. This means, that if you need to wake at 6 am, you should be sleeping by 11:00 PM. That doesn't seem to be an impossible task for most adults. But let's look at school-aged brains.

The average high-school student needs 8.5 hours of sleep per night. A middle schooler, 10 hours. Children in elementary grades first through fourth should be getting about 10.5 hours and preschoolers, 11 hours of sleep.

So a middle school student with a 6:00 wake up time, should be sleeping by 8 o'clock at night!

Average daily sleep needs

age	hours per night
pre-school (3-5 yrs)	11
elementary (5-9 yrs)	10.5
middle school (10-13 yrs)	10
high school (14-18 yrs)	8.5
adults (33-45 yrs)	7

Anyone overriding their brain's own maintenance department is losing out on the opportunity to develop their brains and their intellect to its full capacity. Because most middle and high-school students' bodies are running on an "owl" day rhythm, meaning their bodies have a tendency to stay up late at night and sleep later in the day, it makes it nearly impossible for them to go to bed early enough at night to get all the sleep they need and still wake in time for school.

After all, how many middle school students do you know who can go to sleep at 8:00 at night in order to be rested for a 6:00 am wake up time?

How many of America's students are sleep deprived? Ask yourself, at your school, what percentage of students woke up this morning by artificial means, i.e.: alarm clocks, parents, siblings?   That's the percentage of students in your school who are not getting the rest they need. A bit frightening I think.

One of the ways you can watch for serious sleep deprivation in your own brain is to watch for an event called "**REM Rebound**." This is a bit of a panic attack on the part of your brain and indicates that you probably are pretty seriously deprived of sleep.

REM Rebound is the event of dreaming immediately upon falling asleep. You may notice it when you fall asleep at some inopportune time during the day - say a faculty meeting. You may just nod off for a minute or two and upon waking you realize you have already had a dream.

Remember that in a well maintained brain, it should take you 90 minutes to get to your first dream.   Ninety minutes! - that's an hour and a half. If you dream sooner than this or immediately upon falling asleep that is your body's danger sign. This indicates that your brain is in serious need of maintenance and you need to be more careful about getting your sleep. Unfortunately most people have experienced this at some point in their lives.

Research done at Brown University's medical school just a few years ago looked at the issue of sleep deprivation and found that more than half of high school students went into a REM state 3 minutes after falling asleep - a disturbing statistic given that these are the very same students we are working so hard with during the day hours to improve their brains neural networks.

The research so far has been so unsettling that many sleep researchers are going so far as to accuse school districts, with early high school start times, of child abuse.

The word is getting out, albeit very slowly to school districts and school boards. But in the meantime, what's a parent to do? Most of us know what a struggle it is to get our adolescent children in bed at night at a reasonable time. And we know the struggle of trying to pry them out of it again at the crack of dawn for school.

One suggestion is to have your child keep a sleep log during the month of July (not a bad idea for teachers as well). During the month of July, most children are pretty much on their own time schedule. They go to bed and get up on their own natural clock. Have the child log the bed time and wake-up time for several weeks. An average should emerge. Then compare this "natural" sleep need for what the child actually gets during the school year. It won't solve all the problems but it certainly is a good starting point for discussion.

Sleep journal

day	Mon	Tues	Wed	Thur	Fri	Sat	Sun
bed-time							
woke							
# hrs							

A New Look at Some Old Disabilities

One of the early studies to link night time activity to day time functioning in the brain was a study in New Mexico in the early 1990's led by researcher Jeffrey Lewine. During a experimental brain-imaging study of a young boy with autism, the researchers noticed some very small seizure activity in the child's brain during sleep. What intrigued them was that the activity was on the superior surface of the temporal lobe - the area responsible for language acquisition and social skill interaction.

Given that these are the two hallmarks of autism, the research team was intrigued enough to look at the issue further. They brought 22 children into the center, all with late-onset autism, put them in the same 24 hour **MEG** imaging device and amazingly found that 21 out of the 22 children were having similar seizure activity during sleep.

You can understand what may happen if random electrical activity occurred in neurons and dendrites which really should not be used at all. Imagine thousands of neurons and dendrites that are not being used, getting in the way, causing conflicting thought patterns, and should be removed during routine pruning sessions. What happens though, if these neurons get used accidently through seizure activity in sleep. The brain maintenance system now fails. Neurons which should be removed are kept. This creates huge conflicting brain signals in children with autism. Until new imaging techniques were available, no one would have ever suspected autism may in fact be related to epilepsy.

But what researchers are now beginning to understand is that not only is it important to branch and develop neurons in the brain, but it is equally important to remove certain ones as well. What apparently is happening in the brains of these children with autism is that night time seizure activity is allowing some neurons in their brain to remain when in fact they should be removed as they get in the way of normal wiring. They act then as neuronal roadblocks, shutting down certain vital connections.

The same research team has since found a similar event in the brains of children with a type of dyslexia known as Scotopic Sensitivity Syndrome, sometimes known as Irlen syndrome. This is a type of dyslexia where children struggle with reading, but are greatly assisted by having a colored transparency placed over their reading material.

Apparently the brain maintenance problems are similar here as to what was found in the autistic brain, but in a different region. Small seizure activity during sleep was found in the occipital region of the brains of these children. The inappropriate electrical activity is thought to maintain neurons that should have been removed and cause conflict in the way the brain has wired.

So here were two pieces of very significant research that really emphasized that what happens during sleep can tremendously impact the way a brain functions during the daytime hours. My personal hunch is that most learning disabilities may be caused from some type of night time maintenance problems. I see such a strong relationship between learning disabilities and sleep. One of the most common reports you hear from parents of children with learning disabilities is *"my child doesn't sleep right - my child won't fall asleep - my child won't stay asleep"*. It seems like sleep problems and learning disabilities have gone hand in hand.

There is now similar research on so called "non-disabled" brains which further supports the idea of normal sleep patterns. A research team in Australia showed that children who snore, have lower IQ's than children who do not. Apparently anything you do to disturb the sleep cycle, can disturb the way the brain is wired.

So is sleep an important aspect in learning? Absolutely. Do sleep deprived children do poorer in school? Yes. In fact sleep deprivation has been linked to more than just poor grades and poor testing. It has also been linked to depression, attention deficit disorder emotional instability and memory problems.

How can you tell if your students are sleep deprived? There are a few tests. The easiest is to have them lay their heads down in a darkened room during the day for 7 minutes. Anyone who is asleep at the end of the time period is sleep deprived. (Of course, this might be tough for the teacher as you have to stay awake yourself to time the test!).

.

NOTES

Chapter Nine

Brain Plasticity

All of this wiring and re-wiring throughout childhood and even throughout adulthood is referred to as plasticity. The brain is this fabulous, fluid organ that is changing constantly throughout our lives. It is shaped by our environment, our thoughts, our emotions, and the people in our world.

I'm not sure educators and parents understand what a fluid vehicle we have before us in young people. And the young brain in particular has a great deal of plasticity. We look in any human biology text and it will cover the functions and regions of the brain. It will show that the occipital region is responsible for vision, Broca's region for speech, temporal lobes for auditory processing, etc. However, that's just the default location. That is if nothing stands in the way, a brain will generally put those functions in those areas.

In young brains, the locations for specific activities can really be quite flexible. If one area of the brain is damaged or disabled, any other area of the brain can assume the tasks of that region. The older the brain gets the more difficult it is to achieve that flexibility Keep in mind, that we start with a grand surplus of material in the brain. Of the original 525 billion neurons, we only keep about 20% of them into adulthood. That's a fantastic safety net. We literally throw out 80% of the cells in our brain during childhood. It makes you wonder sometimes if you threw away the right ones, doesn't it?

What determines which ones we keep and which ones we throw away? As we saw in the last chapter, the brain keeps the ones we are using and tosses out the ones we don't. I'm not sure that education has traditionally grasped this concept. I'm not sure we always encourage students to keep the strong cells and leave the weaker ones alone so they can be removed. In fact, what we frequently do is ask students who have a disability in one region to just keep practicing that disabled skill, over and over and over. Are we in fact saying to them, "I can see this area is no good, let's make sure we keep it!"

Would we be better off to tell them to leave it alone, and focus on the areas that are working. Can't we teach the information through the working neurons to strengthen those pathways. Can't we find alternate strategies and ways for them to learn that may utilize a better choice of neurons?

I first became interested in brain plasticity on a personal level when my daughter was 12 months old. We were in a serious head-on auto collision with a drunk driver who fell asleep, crossed the highway median at 50 miles per hour and hit us head-on. My daughter was strapped in her carseat in the front seat and the bulk of the car came in on her (this was back in the days when we were told the safest place for our babies was in the front next to mom).

In addition to other injuries, my daughter received a depressed skull fracture and the subsequent brain damage left her without her speech, her hearing, and much of her motor control. The good news to all of this was that she was just 12 months old. That's a very young brain. That's a brain with a great deal of flexibility. When you have a child at this age with that type of head trauma, you have no choice but to put her in a good infant stimulation program. The program, run through the public school system utilized teachers skilled in re-training brain function. Basically they looked for other areas of her brain that were willing to pick up the functions that were lost.

Today, my beautiful daughter speaks, hears, attends a high school for gifted and talented students and is an avid snowboarder. Is that a miraculous recovery? No. That's what the human brain is capable of doing.

The older the brain gets, the more difficult to rewire. An accident and damage of that magnitude done on an older brain would not have the same chance for recovery. Although most of the hard wiring appears to be complete around the age of ten, we are able to learn and develop our brains at any age. Even an 80 year old brain can be reworked, retrained, improved, groomed, and developed.

The process begins long before we enter the world and can continue until the day we leave it. The neurons are there, and plenty of them. It's up to us what we do with them.

Windows of Opportunity - language

There are certain periods of time in the life of a child, when events and stimuli have a greater influence than at other times. Certain regions of the cortex are at peak construction during various ages. These are termed "**Windows of Opportunity"** because there is a great opportunity at this point to shape the brain.

Some of these windows have been known for quite some time and others are being discovered through new brain imaging research.

One of the earliest windows known was for primary language. The human brain needs to learn some type of language before the age of 10 or 11 or it will most likely never learn language. That's been known for nearly 50 years.

But the window for second languages is very similar. If you are going to learn a second language you really need to be exposed to that language prior to the age of 10. Otherwise you will always struggle with the language and carry your native dialect. There are sounds to that second language you may not be able to hear. Sounds in that language you may not be able to enunciate and it is infinitely more difficult to learn a second language after the age of 10. Now that research has been out for several decades and yet education has failed to accommodate it. We still continue to introduce second languages to children somewhere at the secondary level. It's almost like we are saying to them: "*well now that your window has closed, would you care to learn French?*"

This doesn't mean that we have to have full scale second language programs from elementary school on. But we could at least play tapes and recording of languages, spoken by native speakers, to students at young ages so that at least their brain begins some pathway for the language.

Most people in the United States, if asked which second language would be easiest to learn, will tell you Spanish. It's not really that Spanish is a particularly easy language. It's just relatively easy for Americans because it is probably the only foreign language we heard spoken prior to the age of 10. Even if it was just on Sesame Street, most children in the US have the opportunity to hear Spanish so it is an easier language for us to learn later in life.

Children in Europe who grew up hearing many, many languages spoken due to the geographical proximity to those native countries, tend to find it easier to pick up second languages. Americans have been criticized for years as being mono-linguistic to a fault. I'm not sure that it is so much an attitude problem we have as it is that we are not exposed to many languages as children and our brains are not wired to learn them easily.

Math

One of the other windows of opportunity I mentioned earlier in this book and that is the math and logical reasoning window. The cortex tends to be concentrating on developing that region somewhere between birth and four years of age. Now most of us are not into playing a lot of math games with a 2 year old, but we are in luck in that music will stimulate that same region.

So playing music to young children should help stimulate the region of the brain that they will be using later in life for reasoning activities. I'm often asked what type of music is best (especially after the "Mozart effect" became so popular). My advice is to offer a wide range of music - opera, rap, jazz, rock, punk, classical, and even musical styles which may seem foreign to your ear such as music from distant cultures.

Gross Motor Development

The window of opportunity for motor development appears to be between the ages of birth and 6 years. So children at this age need lots of opportunities to move - on a large scale.

This seems like common sense to anyone who has spent any time around young children. They love to move. They run, they climb, they jump, they slide. These are all activities that don't appeal to many of us older than that age. To me, running up and down my livingroom entryway steps for a half an hour would not be my idea of "fun." For my five year old, it is.

One of the places we see problems in the motor development region is in some lower socio-economic neighborhoods with poor quality child care. Due to economic issues, children in these neighborhoods often spend long days, from an early age, in daycare environments. Some of these daycare settings are very limited in terms of running, climbing, playing opportunities. Some of these environments tend to focus more on sedentary activities in front of television, video, computer games, etc. and children may not have the opportunities to develop these regions as fully as they should.

Vocabulary

The window of opportunity for vocabulary is birth to three years. This means that your cortex decides what percentage it is going to dedicate to vocabulary by your third birthday. So a child in a very rich vocabulary household dedicates a large portion of his cortex. Conversely, a child from a household with a very limited vocabulary dedicates a very small percentage of her cortex.

The national center for child development has found in their recent longitudinal study, that this issue of vocabulary enrichment is the number one factor that correlates to reading success. Children who have a rich vocabulary by age three tend to be good readers. Children who do not have a rich vocabulary, do not. Unfortunately this also correlates strongly with socio-economic status and is one of the arguments for government sponsored early child development centers and programs such as Head-Start in low SES neighborhoods.

It is important to remember that these windows of opportunity do not ever close completely. It is never too late to help someone grow branches, develop skills, improve performance. The windows are just there to remind us of critical time periods where educators and parents can have the most influence on development.

People at all ages can improve language ability, math skills, musical talents, etc. In fact, to ward off the effects of old-age the research is suggesting that we do just that. Try to learn something new everyday. Keep your mind active. Try new things. Get involved in areas outside of your standard conduct. The brain maintains its plasticity throughout life.

Chapter Ten

Memory Systems

I'd like to conclude the main portion of this book with a discussion of memory systems. After all, the real key to teaching is trying to help students put things into their memory system and then hopefully retrieve them out again at some future time and place.

There are generally three steps to storing things into your **memory system**. Problems can occur at any of these three steps. Step one to putting something into your memory is just exposing one of your senses to it. In other words you need to see it, touch it, smell it, hear it, or taste it.

Obviously you can't remember the taste of an orange if you've never tasted one. So this is fairly straight forward. Except for one component. You have to be paying attention to the stimuli. This too seems obvious, but creates a big problem in education. A teacher can lecture on the Battle of Gettysburg during a history class, but if my mind was thinking about a date I had last week-end, then I'm not likely to be storing the Battle of Gettysburg into my head.

As mentioned in an early chapter, this processing or "noticing" task is handled by the Reticular Activating System. In children with attention deficit disorder, here is the first stumbling block to learning. But for all students, attention is a big issue in learning. If they are not attending to the task, it's not going to be processed by the brain and its memory.

Pathway into Memory Storage:
Sensory Input
Short term Memory
Long term Memory

Short Term Memory

Assuming though that you did notice the stimuli, the second step to memory is what is called **short term memory**. What you need to remember about short term memory is that it is very, very short. Short term memory refers to the material that the pre-frontal cortex is currently dealing with. As information comes into the brain, it heads first to the pre-frontal cortex and will mull around there for just a matter of seconds. Short term memory lasts about 20 seconds. After that it is either lost forever, or moves into a long term memory category.

During that 20 second time frame, your brain has a few options at its disposal. It can simply discard the material, never to be recalled again. A good example here would be the cars you pass on your way to work. You stop at a red light, you casually glance at the car next to you, but by the time you get to work, you have no recollection of the car. The vast majority of the material that flows through our lives does not get stored. We select a mere fraction of information to store.

Another choice of the short term memory is to "dump" the information somewhere before throwing it out of the mind. Taking lecture notes in school is a good example of this. You dump the information on paper, then toss it from your head, but know it is written there for future reference.

Long Term Memory

A third option for short term memory is to tag the information as something you wish to store for a longer period of time. These are the things you are going to put into **long term memory**. At this point your brain labels it, puts it in a category, and then begins the long process of cross-referencing the material.

The categorization of the information occurs rather quickly and is handled by the hippocampus. Items are set in categories, sometimes as simple as "things I learned in Mrs. Hayward's art class." But it must go in some type of category. If you have no category, it can't be stored.

Once the hippocampus stores it in a category, the brain will begin its natural process of cross referencing the new items to previous items in other categories. This is the job of the cortex. The cortex is designed to look for patterns and relationships. This takes minutes, hours, days and years. In fact it lasts your whole life and is the reason that learning is so much more fun as you get older. The older person has a wealth of established categories to cross reference to new material.

Basically, the hippocampus memorizes while the cortex learns. There is a difference between memorizing and learning. Memorizing refers to simple recall within one category -

e.g. *The word* **Green** *in Spanish is* **Verde.**

That's memory. It is fairly quick and handled at the sub-cortical level of the brain - the hippocampus. Learning refers to patterns, relationships and cross-references. It takes a long time and is handled at the cortical level (cortex).

> *e. g. - Mesa* **Verde** *is an Indian ruin I visited as a child. The Indians must have thought it looked green. Salsa* **verde** *is always kept on the dinner table at my in-laws house, though I don't care much for*

*the taste. Chile **verde** burritos are served at our favorite restaurant and are very popular in Utah restaurants, though I don't see them as popular in other Mexican restaurants around the US. In Spanish, they put the color after the word it described. In English we wouldn't say burrito green, we would say green burrito. I wonder if other language do it the same as Spanish? Probably, because in Paris, I noticed the sign read "tour Eiffel" not Eiffel Tower.......*

The mental wanderings above are a sample of what the cortex does with the word "verde" versus what the hippocampus does with it. You can see that the cortex is never finished with any item. It just goes on, and on, and on.

Material that is "played with" in this fashion by the brain then becomes a **crystallized memory** as opposed to those things you knew for a month or two and have since forgot.

Retrieval

Interestingly, it is the cross-references that often play a role in the retrieval of information from our memories. It is a natural tendency for the cortex to cross-reference. And yet, here is another area that I think educators over look on a big scale. We don't help students find the cross references, usually because we think they are irrelevant.

I remember doing a workshop in California once where we were doing a little memory game with some teachers. During the demonstration I asked one of the teachers to name three famous painters. She sat there, silent, while all her colleagues looked on. The longer she sat the worse she felt as everyone waited. Finally her eyes rolled up into her head and she said, *"Oh, what were the names of those Ninja Turtles?!"*

We can see what this woman was trying to do. As a retrieval cue, she was going to pull the information out of a cross-reference - a very common retrieval method. She couldn't think of painters, but she remembered that the Ninja Turtle cartoon characters were named after famous painters, so if she could find the Ninja Turtles in her head, then she'd have the painters. It makes perfect sense. We all do this every day.

And yet we don't help our students do the very same thing. When we are teaching a concept in class, do we point out the things they can hook it to? Frequently not, because we think they are irrelevant and distract from our topic.

If I teach about the early explorer Cortez, do I also mention that it is a city in Colorado near the four corners area that is the king of pinto beans? Probably not. Why? Because I think that's irrelevant. But yet, regardless of how silly and unrelated some things seem, students, just like you and I will frequently retrieve information via a cross reference rather than the category and circumstance under which it was first learned.

Types of Memory

Another area which really assists students is to cross reference information between their two major memory systems. We actually have three different memory systems in our brain. **Procedural memory**, which tends to be housed in our spinal cord, was mentioned in the early part of this book. **Episodic memory**, which is your autobiographical memory (think, episodes of your life). And lastly, **semantic memory**, which is the memory where you stored intentionally learned information.

What is interesting about the different memories is not so much that they are separate, but the difference in the control we have over each. Semantic memory is generally under our complete control. We decide if something will be stored or not. A teacher gives you a list of terms, tells you to learn them, you agree, and then study them. That's semantic memory.

The problem with it, is the student can just as easily decline. The teacher can give you the terms, tell you to learn them, you do not agree, and you don't study them.

As most of us in education know, that happens much more often than we'd like. We tell the students to learn something, even tell them it is important and will be on the test. But, alas, the child doesn't seem to feel the same great desire we do and so they choose not to learn.

Now let's look at episodic memory. Here you have no control. You do not decide whether or not something is stored in your episodic memory - it just happens. Can you remember the last time you saw your father? Do you remember the weather yesterday? Do you remember the last thing you baked in your oven? I'll bet if I asked you about the last meal you ate you could describe it in great detail including where you ate it, who you ate with and the color of the utensils. And yet, no one told you to learn it. No one told you it was important or that it would be on the test. Furthermore, you remember it whether you wanted to or not. We can't control what is stored in our episodic memory. It just happens.

We spend the majority of our time in the classroom trying to teach to a student's semantic memory. This is frustrating because sometimes the student refuses to learn and remember. How much easier our job would be if we could teach to the episodic memory! Now the student will learn and remember whether they want to or not. Now the learning is within the teacher's control.

When we teach to the episodic memory in education they call it "hands-on" learning or "experiential" learning. The advantage to hands-on learning is that it teaches to the episodic memory system as opposed to the semantic.

Unfortunately teaching to the episodic memory system is time consuming, so we can't teach absolutely everything through this system during the school year. It would take too long. So ideally, you can teach the bulk of the material to the semantic and then cross reference all that to the episodic.

To add even more strength to an episodic memory, hook an emotional component to it. Now it is set for life. I'm not exaggerating here. If you store something in your episodic memory and it has an emotional component, you will store it for the rest of your life.

Want Proof? Can you remember taking high school biology? Think hard. Is there a memory there? I'll bet it has something to do with frogs, doesn't it? Now, do you remember your wedding day? (Yes, it's unrelated to the frogs) Do you remember giving birth? Do you remember the first time you saw your son or daughter? Do you remember where you were when you heard about the Oklahoma City bombing? Do you remember where you were when you saw a plane fly into the World Trade Center?

These are called flashbulb memories. They are episodic memories with an emotional attachment. They are the strongest memories we have and the most durable.

When designing Layered Curriculum™, this very issue is the point behind the "B" layer. It provides an episodic experience, preferably with an emotional component, to which students can cross reference all the other material. Because of time constraints, we must teach a lot of information to the semantic memory (this comprises the "C" layer in Layered Curriculum™) and then cross reference it to a funny, disgusting, or weird emotional personal experience. (See appendix for overview on Layered Curriculum™)

Memory Retrieval Problems & Solutions

Storing information into the memory is one thing, but retrieving it back out again can be quite a different matter. Many of the issues of retrieval revolve around problems in the storage. If something has been stored in an easily identifiable category, and has sufficient cross references, you should be able to retrieve it back out again. But as many of us know, retrieval failure is a frustrating and common situation.

By far, the biggest obstacle to memory retrieval is stress. I can't emphasize enough how disastrous stress is for the memory system. We simply cannot access our memories under stress. Educators need to use stress like most people use garlic. A little is a nice touch, but no one wants a garlic sandwich!

A little stress in the learning process is nice. It adds a little interest and motivation and encourages children to learn. But stress is only good in very tiny quantities.

Moderate or severe stress is horrid for the brain. It releases chemicals which literally cause the neurons in the hippocampus to atrophy and die. Chronic stress during childhood can create permanent changes in the neurotransmitter levels in the brain. And it is physically impossible to retrieve information out of our memory while under stress.

Everyone has seen the pain on Johnny's face when called on in class to answer a simple question. But with everyone watching and some classmates snickering, it very quickly becomes impossible for Johnny to even think of his best friend's name, let alone the correct answer. Of course once the teacher leaves Johnny, and moves on to Shira, now Johnny can think of 100 answers he should have given.

I can remember sitting in a test in college looking at a question that was very familiar. I had spent a long time studying the material and I knew that the answer was somewhere in my head, but I sure couldn't access it. Of course, as soon as I turned in the test and walked out the door, the answer was clear in my memory.

Be very aware of stress in the classroom. Obviously we cannot remove all stress from life, nor should we. But to add additional stress just for the sake of it, is cruel and has no place in school or any learning situation. Students need to feel comfortable and free to take risks so that they can access the creative higher level thinking parts of their brains.

Often times memory retrieval is just linked to insufficient cross references. Help students find cross references and make them silly. Humor is a fabulous emotion to help strengthen memories. Fun, silly, and bizarre cross references are the best because they hook the emotion to the memory.

Make sure students are asked to retrieve information in the same environment they learned it in. Want to quickly increase test scores? Test students in the same room they were prepared in. As a high school teacher I really saw this in Advanced Placement testing. We would prep the kids all year in our room. And then on test day, they wanted to move them all to the library for their test! No way. Not on my watch.

I'm referring here to cue-triggered recall. It's another *biggie* in terms of memory retrieval. You and I use it all the time. You are standing in the kitchen unloading groceries when suddenly you remember something you forgot to do in your family office. So you drop everything, rush down the hall to the office - and stand there like a stump. You have absolutely no idea why you are here? What was it you needed in the office?

What do we do at this point? We go back to the kitchen where we were unloading groceries and look around for the visual field we saw when that thought entered our heads -*"Oh - yeah, now I know what I needed to do!"* It's called cue-triggered recall. It is the purpose behind mentally "re-tracing your steps" to find a lost item. We use it all the time as a retrieval aid.

And yet when we prepare students all year for an exam and them move them to another room on test day, we are depriving them of this very important memory device. Don't let them do that to your students.

Chapter Eleven

Frequently Asked Questions-
Real questions from real teachers.

Q: Kathie, Is there really a difference between men's brains and women's brains?

A: This always sounds like a loaded question to me. I know I'm going to be used as fuel for some argument at the dinner table, but, here goes. Is there a difference between male and female brains? From a practical standpoint, no. There are such greater differences between individuals of both genders that there really are no clear differences that characterize a man or a woman.

There are a few differences however and since the male/female thing seems to be a fun topic for debate I'll give them to you.

There are two general types of brains. We call them *male differentiated* and *female differentiated* because most (but not all) male have the first and most females (but not all) have the second. In the male differentiated brain, the neurons are more densely packed and the cortex hemispheres tend to be the same size. In the female differentiated brain, the left hemisphere cortex is thicker than the right. There is also a thicker corpus callosum in this brain.

The biggest difference between the two brain types is in the hypothalamus. It tends to be larger in male differentiated brains than in the female type - generally considered to be the product of testosterone on the developing embryo

Another significant area of difference is in the area of language. Male differentiated brains tend to limit language to the left hemisphere whereas female differentiated utilize both halves of the brain for language. The left hemisphere's "language area" is also quite sophisticated and highly developed in the female differentiated brain. The male differentiated brain tends to have a highly developed area in the right hemisphere used for visual spacial coordination.

There are some chemical differences as well. Besides the sex hormone differences, women tend to have less serotonin than men - a problem linked to depression occurring more frequently in women.

But here again, we can't assume all these items separate the sexes. Only 80% of men have a male differentiated brain and only about the same percentage of women have the female differentiated. Your physical gender doesn't guarantee your brain gender. It all had to do with hormone levels produced by your birth mother during her pregnancy with you.

Q: Kathie, does television violence make children more prone to violence? Does it change their brains?

A: The television violence topic really deals with two issues. The first issue regards the effect of violent cartoons on early elementary grade children. We've heard for years from parents and elementary teachers that shows like Power Rangers, Ninja Turtles, Poke' Mon and the like were making children violent.

Truthfully, I believe this is an instance of the programming following the child, not the other way around. Violent behavior tends to peak in children between age 5 and 7. This is a violent period. Children at this age love to shoot, blow-up, karate chop, and explode all types of imaginary and unfortunately sometimes not so imaginary characters and "enemies".

These types of cartoons are so appealing to this age group because they speak their language. I'm not sure we'd have calmer 6 years without the programs. Of course, he's another opportunity for the adults in their world to model alternate strategies for dealing with emotions. As tempting as it may be, don't "karate chop" them back.

Now the other issue of violence on television is cause for concern. That's the issue of how we have become desensitized to murder, death and all types of previously horrific activities. The research shows that while watching television violence won't necessarily make an adolescent violent, it does de-sensitize them to the emotions we associate with it. Personally, I try to really limit the amount my children are exposed to.

Q: Where does love fit in the brain?

A: There has been some very interesting new findings on the biology of love. They link attraction between humans to the chemical **oxytocin**. Now the discovery of oxytocin is certainly not new. We've known about it for years - it's the hormone associated with milk secretion in mammals. But what is new is its association with attachment. Apparently monogamous animals have this chemical, oxytocin in their brains. Promiscuous animals do not. Some researchers discovered that they could inject oxytocin into the brains of promiscuous animals and suddenly, viola' they would form attachments to each other.

When the research went further, they found that oxytocin concentrations actually change location in the brain based on the type of relationship we have with another person. During new love - that exciting, dynamic, can't-keep-my-hands-off-you kind of love - the oxytocin is located down in the reptilian brain. This probably explains the reason those relationships are so fun. When the relationship matures (25 years of marriage later) the oxytocin has now migrated up into the cortex of the brain. Mature relationships, while maybe not as "fun" certainly are much more logical.

So researchers are now looking at oxytocin levels and trying to link this possibly to problems with attachment. All humans, male and female have oxytocin. It bonds us to each other as friends, parents, lovers, and grandparents. Is it possible that some people just don't produce enough of this and it leads to problems with attachment? We'll have to wait to find out.

Q: Are there some things I can do to raise the IQ of my child?

A: Absolutely. I think there is a great deal a parent or teacher can do to influence the IQ of a child. IQ, or intelligence is certainly not a stable thing. It is very fluid and can change significantly over the course of your life, particularly during childhood.

The plan of action you take depends on the age of the child. We affect intelligence differently at different ages. During infancy one of the key boosts you can do for your child's IQ is breast feed. Breast fed babies grow up to be more intelligent adults than bottle fed babies. There is a substance in breast milk that helps myelinate the central nervous system faster. Remember myelin is that fatty covering that causes nerve cells to fire at a much faster rate. Breast fed babies' central nervous systems develop at a faster rate and they can process information from their environments at a faster rate. The substance, to date, has not been replicated in packaged baby formula. There are some new formulas out now which advertise they are adding this, but the research has been controversial as to whether or not they can really duplicate the action.

Aside from breast feeding, another thing you can do with your infant is to develop a mini - "infant stimulation program" for them. You just want to expose them to a wide variety of sensory stimuli. So change the mobile over their bed once a week. Hang different pictures with bold shapes next to the crib. Play music for them - different types of music. Buy their pajamas in a variety of fabrics with various textures - terry, cotton, satin, etc. You don't want to overwhelm the child. They need plenty of sleep and downtime, but during the times they are awake, give them a variety of stimuli to experience rather than just the same old thing everyday. And as they get older, use a wide vocabulary with them. Vocabulary enrichment by age 3 is critical.

For pre-school age children you want to work on the area of "adapting themselves to different situations." This is the beginning of problem solving - one of the keys to intelligence. So, take them places. All kinds of places. Take them places where they have to adapt to the situation. Take them to different kinds of restaurants, to the mall, (different malls) take them on a road trip, a plane trip, to the fire station, to church, to Grandma's house. If you work with this age group, think *field trips*! And lots of them.

Every time the children go to a new place they are operating outside of their spinal cord and lower regions. This means they are using their cortex, firing neurons, building branches.   (This is why traveling to foreign countries is so exhausting for adults - you have to *think* about everything, nothing is routine. It's tiring - but good for the brain.)

For the school age child - school is pretty stimulating. As long as you ensure that they are thinking through projects and you hold them accountable for the day to day learning experience, school does a pretty good job of stimulating the brain.

For the adult - use your brain. Learn new things every day. Travel. Go to new places. Take courses at your community college.   Just challenge yourself a bit. Remember the brain is a use-it-or-lose-it machine.

Q: Kathie, we're seeing more and more students in our school with the diagnosis of Asperger syndrome or high functioning Autism. What is causing the increase and what is the difference between those two labels?

A: You're talking about two categories which fall under a much broader category of disabilities called **Pervasive Developmental Disorders**, or PDD. In addition to Autism and Asperger syndrome, you also find Tourette's syndrome and the really swell label of PDD-NOS (Pervasive Developmental Disorder, Not Otherwise

Specified - the ultimate generic label) in this broad category.

We do see these students in higher numbers these days because professionals are now coming to see that many more children than previously thought, fit into the category. It used to be traditionally reserved for children who had fairly moderate to profound mental retardation. But today we see that many children without mental retardation fit in the category because of language and or social dysfunction.

The terms "high-functioning Autism," "Asperger syndrome" and the new term "Autism without Mental Retardation" do not have firm boundaries. Even the experts in the field cannot agree on where one starts and the other stops. You can get all three diagnoses on the same child from three different professionals, so it's no wonder parents and educators are confused.

In general, both Autism and Asperger syndrome indicate a significant delay in both language and social skills with a narrow, intense focus of interest. Autism generally has a larger language delay than Aspergers, but again, exceptions rule.

Most diagnosticians look for the degree to which the child lacks a "sense of self" or the understanding that I have thoughts and feelings and you have thoughts and feelings and they may not be the same. Children with Autism have less of a sense of self. Children with Autism also tend to process faces and objects in the same region of the brain while non-autistic individuals separate those two tasks.

However, that said, the categories overlap considerably and it doesn't really make a difference which label the child uses as these children are so unique that individual plans are designed one-on-one anyway. My suggestion to parents is that if you have professionals that will go either way - Asperger's or high-functioning Autism, take the Autism label. It tends to give you more legal protection than Asperger's Syndrome.

Q: I'm working with a young boy of 10 who I think may have dyslexia because his reading problems are so pronounced. But I'm not really clear on what dyslexia is. Can you clarify?

A: Here's another area that even the experts can't agree on. What causes dyslexia? What areas of the brain are involved in dyslexia? How to treat dyslexia? These are all hot areas of current research.

When most people think of dyslexia they think of letter and word reversals - seeing "b" instead of "d," etc. But that's a very small percentage of dyslexic students. If a child is reading very much below their age and significantly lower than their IQ indicates they should be reading, dyslexia is a good guess for blame.

In other words if the child has a normal or high IQ, has no obvious visual problems, appeared to develop rather normally without significant emotional trauma or other factor, then that's the typical dyslexic child.

The brain research indicates it is a problem in the language-related visual input process. These children have trouble with short term memory, storage, and phonemic awareness. Many times the child can learn the sounds of all the letters but has serious problems "memorizing" sight words. This means that every time she sees the word "tree" she has to sound it out because unlike you and I she doesn't just pull the thing out of memory as a sight word. They tend to write everything very phonetically.

Some children process the language in the right hemisphere rather than the left. It is debated whether the problems come from that or that their brain had problems in the left hemisphere all along, so just moved language to the right side.

Some children as I mentioned in Chapter eight, have neuron weeding problems in the occipital lobe which causes the Irlen syndrome I described. The colored lenses or transparencies can offer assistance for them.

Different therapies and treatments have varied success in different children. I always suggest finding a good reading tutor who is schooled in a variety of choices and can see which ones have the most success for the individual.

Q.: Kathie, How does all this translate into the classroom?

A: I really appreciate this question because I've spent the last 10 years working on the answer! You can really boil all the research down to four key educational principles. First and foremost, we have to move students up to higher regions of their brain on day to day school and homework.

As I mentioned earlier, educators, myself included, have focused far too much effort on process accountability rather than product accountability. We only cared if students "did" the assignment, not necessarily whether they "learned" the assignment.

Sometimes "doing" an assignment just means you have enough friends. Anyone can "do" the assignment. But we need to shift our focus onto the learning. We need to say to the students "here's what I need you to learn" and then give them suggestions on how to do that. But the ultimate goal is the learning.

The second issue I see coming out of brain research is the issue of attention. We now have a much better understanding of what focuses attention and problems that relate to attention. If the child is not attending to the work, they are not going to learn. The best way I've found to have them attend is through the perception of "self-made choice."   (See Layered Curriculum™ appendix).

The third big issue is that we now understand the power behind *the Reptilian Brain* and its battle for control. Everyone wants some control. If you don't give it to them, they will take it. That's the beauty behind any type of "student-centered learning." It puts the student in control of what they are doing and really soothes the savage beast.

The fourth issue has to do with the development and plasticity of the cortex. Perhaps we need to really focus on helping students grow branches. Lots and lots of beautiful branched network webbing together regions of the cortex and areas between the cortex and lower areas.

Those four keys are the cornerstones to Layered Curriculum™. It is designed to work "with" the student's brain rather than against it. More information is available at the Layered Curriculum™ website: http://Help4Teachers.com and in the appendix following this chapter.

Appendix A :

Layered Curriculum™

Layered Curriculum™ is a teaching method which combines all the latest information on the brain with the realities of the classroom. If you feel like a circus performer trying to juggle learning styles, mind styles, intelligences, abilities and exceptionalities all while covering the content, you are not alone.

Layered Curriculum™ incorporates the four key elements of the brain:
- priority of lower regions
- catching a student's attention
- over-riding the power of the reptilian brain
- the biology of neuron branching in the cortex

and creates a simple model of student-centered instruction that works at all grade levels, elementary through adult education. Here are the basic steps to Layered Curriculum.

Step One: Divide what you need to teach into three categories based on the complexity of thinking. Categories are basic content, application/manipulation, critical analysis.

Step Two: Design a variety of assignment choices for each of your key objectives.

Step Three: Write your plan down in a simple form to be given to the students. (See 'layers" explanation below)

Step Four: Design a brief rubric for the types of assignments you offer and share that with the students.

Step Five: Discuss all assignments with the students before awarding points to ensure accountability.

The "Layers" of Layered Curriculum™

The bottom layer, called the **C layer** (because students can earn a grade no higher than a C from this layer) includes basic content, rote memorization, practice, direct instruction (think about the lower levels of Bloom's taxonomy).

Students choose from a variety of assignment choices in this C layer. The more diverse your student population, the more variety you need in the C layer. Different assignments are worth different points based on their complexity. Offer a menu which includes about three times as many assignments as you require the students to do.

The second layer, called the **B layer** (because students who want a B will move into this layer after finishing the C layer) contains assignment choices which allow the student to "play" with the concepts learned in the C layer. This layer includes application, manipulation, problem solving, etc.

The top layer, called the **A layer** (because students who want a grade of A will move into this layer after finishing the B layer), contains assignments which require the highest kind of thinking - critical thinking.

This section contains questions for student debate. Students will be mixing research with things not found in research such as morals, values, ethics, and personal opinion. The opinion is generally presented in the form of a written opinion.

The Key's to Layered Curriculum™

Key One: Hold students accountable for learning. This is done through a very brief oral defense of assignments. Students are awarded points based on what they *learned* rather than what they *did*.

Key Two: Offer choice whenever or where ever possible. Nothing changes the dynamics of a classroom faster than student ownership. Having students choose their assignments and points not only catches their attention, it reduces the "control" battles with the hypothalamus.

Key Three: Encourage higher level thinking. This is done by hooking their class grade into the complexity of thinking. C layer puts things in the memory system of the hippocampus. The B layer encourages the learning process to move through the cortex with cross references. The A layer encourages branches between a wide range of cortical and sub-cortical areas with debate and opinion.

Examples of how Layered Curriculum Units are Designed

A 10th grade biology class Layered Curriculum may have 15 - 20 assignment choices in *the C layer* as the emphasis is on basic content. Assignment choice include lectures, video, art work, vocabulary flash cards, book work, computer work, etc.

The B layer may contain a selection of 2 or 3 lab choices where students are presented a problem they need to solve such as whether the temperature of water will affect plant growth.

The A layer may contain 2 or 3 questions of debate among current events on the topic. Perhaps an question as to whether or not genetically altered plants are safe to eat.

In this class *the C layer* has the bulk of the points as the state assessment requires a great deal of basic content knowledge.

A middle school art class Layered Curriculum may have just a few assignments in *the C layer* as the students learn the basics of the use of color. There will be some direct instruction and maybe an assignment or two.

The B layer will be quite weighty as application is the main focus of this course. Students are given some choice in an art project demonstrating the skills of the unit.

The A layer is also rather small, but important. It may ask students to find some art in their community - perhaps tying it in to a field trip to the city/county courthouse, where they evaluate the use of color in the building.

NOTES

Appendix B:

The Biochemistry of Neurotransmitters
(a simple story)

Neurotransmitters are either made FROM amino acids or actually ARE amino acids. The neurotransmitters that ARE amino acids are:

- glutamate
- aspartate
- glycine
- gamma-aminobutyric acid (GABA) - this one is actually a slight modification of glutamate.

The rest (see exception below) of the neurotransmitters are made FROM amino acids. But there are only two amino acids to choose from: Tyrosine or Tryptophan. Since they are made from one single amino acid, they are given the appropriate name: **Monoamine Neurotransmitters**

If they are made from tyrosine, they are called catecholamines:

- dopamine
- norepinephrine
- epinephrine

If they are made from tryptophan they are called indolamines:

• serotonin

The design of them is quite simple. Most neurons can take tyrosine and turn it into L-DOPA. And they are also talented enough to turn L-DOPA into dopamine. TaDa! That sounds easy enough.

Here's where we separate the talented from the truly talented neurons. Some neurons are happy with the dopamine and use it as is. But some neurons, with exceptional skills have enzymes that can actually convert dopamine into norepinephrine. Wow!

Just when you thought you'd seen it all, let me tell you that some neurons are happy with their norepinephrine and use it. But some really, really exceptional neurons (they go to gifted & talented neuron school) have enzymes that can actually convert norepinephrine into epinephrine!

So that's how you make the catecholamines. Some neurons just produce dopamine, some norepinephrine and some epinephrine depending on their talents (and enzyme production).

Serotonin is made by other neurons in a rather lack luster process of turning tryptophan into serotonin.

The Exceptions

There always has to be an exception. Well, in this instance, it's Acetylcholine. As you may suspect, Acetylcholine is a combination of an acetyl group and a choline molecule. If that explanation is sufficient, stop here.

If you need more specific information, an acetyl group is CH_3CO- and a choline molecule is one of the major components in the phospholipids of the cell membrane. It is composed of 3 methyl groups. (CH_3)

Some gases too can act as neurotransmitters in that they can pass through the cell easily and produce a secondary neuron messenger. Nitric oxide and carbon monoxide are two such gases.

NOTES

Glossary

Acetylcholine - Neurotransmitter. Composed of an acetyl group (CH_3CO-) and a choline molecule. Imbalance linked to Alzheimer's Disease

Action potential - The firing of a neuron. Cell membrane becomes permeable to electrical charges.

Agonist.- Any neurotransmitter whose action is to excite a neighboring neuron.

Alzheimer's Disease - The physical separation of the hippocampus from the rest of the brain. Results in serious memory loss.

Amino acid - Building blocks for all proteins.

Amygdala - Small structure in the limbic system of the brain associated with emotions and pleasure.

Antagonist - Any neurotransmitter whose action is to inhibit a neighboring neuron.

Attention deficit disorder - Genetic disorder associated with attention problems. Results from insufficient dopamine secreted in the hind brain and the subsequent loss in blood flow to that region.

Attention deficit/hyperactivity disorder - A disorder combined from attention problems in the hind brain and neurotransmitter imbalance in the peripheral nervous system which causes impulsive behavior.

Autolysis - Self destruction. Associated with enzymes such as Calpain in neurons.

Caffeine - a neurotransmitter mimic which speeds up activity in both the peripheral and central nervous system.

Calpain - Self destructive enzyme found in neurons. Responsible for cell death in infrequently used cells.

Central nervous system (CNS) - The brain and spinal cord.

Cerebral cortex - Top portion of the brain. Composed of a thin tissue, six cell layers thick. It is responsible for higher level thinking in humans.

Crippled brain - Term used to describe the brain of drug addicts who have used substances so long that receptor sites have been damaged and destroyed on the amygdala.

Crystallized memory - Memory that has fired a neural pathway a sufficient number of times to now be able to withstand the test of time.

Dendrites - Branches on neurons which allow for the brain's plasticity.

Dopamine - One of the monoamine neurotransmitters. Responsible for many major brain functions. Dysfunctional levels are responsible for Attention Deficit Disorder, Parkinsons' Disease and a host of other mental problems.

Ecstasy - The street name for the drug MDMA, 3,4-methylenedioxymethamphetamine. Generally taken in tablet form, the drug gives a feeling of euphoria and increased energy. Biologically, it disturbs serotonin and dopamine levels in the limbic system leading to memory loss, obsessive compulsive disorders and other mental disturbances.

Epinephrine - One of the monoamine neurotransmitters. Responsible for fight or flight response, converting glucogen to glucose, and removing fatty acids from fat cells.

Episodic memory - The memory associated with the autobiographical storage of our life.

Frontal lobe - The lobe of the cortex located behind the forehead. Unique to humans, it is associated with planning, organizational skills, language and problem solving.

Habituation - Adaptation to a stimulus at the brain level. The brain's ability to ignore unimportant stimuli.

Hind brain - Primitive lower region of the brain composed of the medulla and the pons.

Hippocampus - A portion of the brain which lies along the line of the limbic system and cortex joining. Responsible for memory formation.

Homeostasis - The body's drive for "sameness." It provides safety and adjustment feature so that the body can correct for imbalances in hormone levels, fluid levels, body temperature, weight, etc.

Hyperactivity disorder - A peripheral nervous system disorder resulting from an underactive nervous system. Impulsive behaviors exhibited are the result of the system's attempt to stimulate itself. Generally found in children under the age of nine.

Hypothalamus - Brain region in the Limbic System responsible for primitive emotions, hunger, body temperature and hormone regulation.

Layered Curriculum™ - Student-centered teaching method designed by Kathie F Nunley. It utilizes a triangular model of instruction. Grades are tied into the complexity of student thinking. Points are given for learning demonstrated through an oral defense.

Limbic system - A name given to the middle portion of the human brain composed of the thalamus, hypothalamus, amygdala, hippocampus and pituitary gland.

MEG - Magnetoencephalography. Brain imaging technique designed to look at minute activity in the cortex.

Monoamine Neurotransmitters. - Any of the neurotransmitters made from a single amino acid, either tryptophan or tyrosine. Dopamine, norepinephrine, epinephrine, and serotonin.

Nerve-blockers - Drugs which inhibit transmission of signals between neurons.

Neuron - A nerve cell.

Neurotransmitters - Chemicals used to carry messages of stimulation between nerve cells.

Occipital lobe - Lobe of brain cortex found at the back of the head. Chiefly responsible for vision.

Oxytocin - Hormone found in mammals and responsible for milk secretion. Recent research has also linked it to bonding in humans.

Parietal lobe - Lobes of brain cortex found at the top of the head. Responsible for most of the incoming sensory information.

Peripheral nervous system (PNS) - Body nerves. Those nerves found outside of the brain and spinal cord.

Pervasive Developmental Disorders - Group of disorders characterized by delays in language and or social skill development. Includes autism, Asperger's syndrome, Tourette's syndrome and PDD-NOS.

Pituitary gland - Gland found in the limbic system of the brain. Responsible for hunger and hormones.

Pre-frontal cortex - Region of cortex found directly behind the forehead. Responsible for decision making.

Procedural memory - Memories associated with muscle actions that are stored in the spinal cord.

Proneurotrophins - Molecules produced when neurotrophins break off from ribosomes too early and can lead to cell death. Association with early cell decay in Alzheimer's Disease.

Punishment - Any consequence which follows a behavior which leads to a decrease in the behavior occurring again.

Re-uptake mechanism - Mechanism found on nerve cells which allows the cell to recapture neurotransmitters from the synapse to be recycled.

Receptor sites - Location on a cell where an enzyme or neurotransmitter can attach.

Reinforcement - Any consequence which follows a behavior which leads to an increase in the behavior occurring again.

REM - Rapid Eye Movement. A stage in the sleep cycle during which most dreaming occurs.

REM Rebound - Dreaming immediately upon falling asleep or within a fast time period. Well maintained brains will dream 90 minutes after falling asleep.

Reptilian brain - A name given to the middle part of the brain encompassing the limbic system. The portion of the brain humans share with the reptilian class of animals.

Resting state - Name given to the state a neuron is in when charges are separate and no electrical activity is firing.

Reticular Activating System (RAS) - Found in the hind brain, the region of the brain which focuses attention.

Semantic memory - Memory system responsible for storing specific facts and information we intentionally want to store.

Serotonin - One of the monoamine neurotransmitter. Synthesized from tryptophan.

Synapse - Space between neurons. Chemical activity occurs here.

Temporal lobe - Lobe of the brain found on the sides of the head. Responsible primarily for hearing and processing language.

Thalamus - Region of the brain responsible for sorting sensory information. Found in the limbic system.

Tyrosine - Amino acid responsible for the production of the neurotransmitters, dopamine, norepinephrine, and epinephrine.

Selected References

Auerbach, J. et al. (2001). DRD4 related to infant attention and information processing: A developmental link to ADHD? *Psychiatric Genetics*, 11(1), 31-35.

Barron. (2000).Problem solving in video-based microworlds: Collaborative and individual outcomes of high-achieving sixth grade students. *Journal of Educational Psychology*, 92, 391-398

Bartzokis, G. et al. (2000). Age-related brain volume changes in amphetamine and cocaine addicts and normal controls: implications for addiction risk? *Psychiatric Research: Neuroimaging*, 98(2), 93-102.

Bennett, P. et al. (2001). Evidence for age-related cortical reorganization. *Acta Psychologica*, 172, 249-273.

Benware & Deci (1984). The quality of learning with an active versus passive motivational set. *American Educational Research Journal*, 21, 755-765.

Bhattacharya, G. (2000). Adjustment of South Asian immigrant children to schools in the United States. *Adolescence*, 35(137), 77-85.

Biederman, J. et al. (2000). Age-Dependent decline of symptoms of Attention Deficit Hyperactivity Disorder: Impact of Remission Definition and Symptom Type. *American Journal of Psychiatry*, 157(5), 816-818.

Binks, et.al. (1999). Short-term total sleep deprivation does not impair cortical functioning. *Sleep*, Vol. 22(3), 328-334.

Blunden, S., et al, (2000). Behaviour and neurocognitive performance in children aged 5–10 years who snore compared to controls, *Journal of Clinical & Experimental Neuropsychology*, 22(5), 554-568.

Boggiano et al., (1993). Use of techniques promoting students' self-determination: Effects on students' analytic problem-solving skills. *Motivation and Emotion,* 17, 319-336.

Bookheimer, S., et al. (2000). Activation of language cortex with automatic speech tasks. *Neurology*, 55(8), 1151-1157.

Born, J., et al. (2000). Early sleep triggers memory for early visual discrimination skills. *Nature Neuroscience*, 3, 1335-39.

Bremner, et al.(2000) Hippocampal volume reduction in major depression. *American Journal of Psychiatry*, 157(1), 115-117.

Burchinal, et.al. (2000). *Relating quality of center-based child care to early cognitive and language development longitudinally. Child Development,* 71(2),338-357

Burgess, C., et al. (2000). Agony & Ecstasy: A review of MDMA effects and toxicity. *European Psychiatry*, 15(5) 287-294.

Byrne, T. et al. (2000). *Pharmacology, Biochemistry & Behavior*, 66(3) 501-508.

Clure, C. et al (1999). Attention-deficit/hyperactivity disorder and substance use: Symptom pattern and drug choice. *American Journal of Drug and Alcohol Abuse*. 25(3), 441-448.

Compton, R. & Mintzer, D. (2001). Effects of worry and evaluation stress on interhemispheric interaction. *Neuropsychology*, 15(4), 427-433.

Corina, D. et al. (2001). fMRI auditory language differences between dyslexic and able reading children. *Neuroreport*, 12(6), 1195-1201.

Curran, et. al., (1999). *American Journal of Psychiatry*. 156(10), 1664-1665.

Deci & Ryan, (1987). The support of autonomy and the control of behavior. *Journal of Personality and Social Psychology*, 53,1024-1037.

Deci, Nezlek, & Sheinman, (1981). Characteristics of the rewarder and intrinsic motivation of the rewardee. *Journal of Personality and Social Psychology*, 40, 1-10.

Deci, Schwartz, et al., (1981). An instrument to assess adults' orientations toward control versus autonomy with children: Reflections on intrinsic motivation and perceived competence. *Journal of Educational Psychology,* 73, 642-650.

Deery, H. (1999). Hazard and risk perception among young novice drivers, *Journal of Safety Research,* 30 (4) 225-236.

DeWolfe, N, et al. (2000). *Journal of Attention Disorders,* 4(2), 80-90.

Duman, et al., (1999). Neural plasticity to stress and antidepressant treatment. *Biological Psychiatry,* 46(9), 1181-1191.

Emilien, et al .(1999) *Irish Journal of Psychological Medicine,* 16(1), 18-23.

Ficca, G., et al. (2000). Sleep organization in the first year of life: developmental trends in the quiet sleep-paradoxical sleep cycle. *Behavioural Brain Research.* 112(1-2), 159-163.

Fishbein, D. (2000)... *Criminal Justice & Behavior,* 27(2), 139-159.

Flink, et al, (1992). Children's achievement-related behaviors: The role of extrinsic and intrinsic motivational orientations. In A. K. Boggiano & T.S. Pittman (Eds.), *Achievement and motivation: a social-developmental perspective* (pp. 189-214). New York: Cambridge University Press.

Frijters, et al. (2000). Direct and mediated influences of home literacy and literacy interest on prereaders' oral vocabulary and early written language skill. *Journal of Educational Psychology*, 92 (3)466-477.

Gais, S. et al. (2000). Early sleep triggers memory for early visual discrimination skills. *Nature Neuroscience* 12, 1335-1339.

Gamma, A, et al. (2001). Posttreatment results of combining naltrexone with cognitive-behavior therapy for the treatment of alcoholism. *Journal of Clinical Psychopharmacology.* 21(1) 66-71.

Gamma, A, et al. (2000). MDMA modulates cortical and limbic brain activity as measured by HS150- pet in healthy humans *Neuropsychopharmacology.* 23(4) 388-395.

Gatz, M. et al. (2001). Education and the risk of Alzheimer's disease: Findings from the study of dementia in Swedish twins. *Journals of Gerontology* 56B(5), 292-300.

Gerra, G. et al. (2000). Long-lasting effects of Ecstasy on serotonin function in humans. *Biological Psychiatry*, 47(2) 127-136.

Glisky, E. et al. (2001). Source memory in older adults: an encoding or retrieval problem? *Journal of Experimental Psychology: Learning, Memory, and Cognition*, 27(5), 1131-1146

Goel, V & Dolan, R. (2001). The functional anatomy of humor: segregating cognitive and affective components. *Nature Neuroscience*, 4(3), 237-238.

Gorman, J. (1997). The Essential Guide to Psychiatric Drugs, 3rd ed. St. Martin's Press, New York.

Gottfried, A. et al. (2001). *Journal of Educational Psychology*, 93(1), 3-13.

Gould, E., et al. (2000). Regulation of Hippocampal neurogenesis in adulthood. *Biological Psychiatry*, 48(9), 715-720.

Gruber, Sadeh, & Raviw. (2000). Instability of sleep patterns in children with attention deficit/hyperactivity disorder. *Journal of the American Academy of Child and Adolescent Psychiatry*, 39(4), 495-501.

Green, et al, (1999). Magnetic resonance imaging study of caudal infrasylvian region reveals novel findings in dyslexia. *Neurology*, 53(5), 974-981

Grolnick & Ryan (1987). Autonomy in children's learning: An experimental and individual difference investigation. *Journal of Personality and Social Psychology*, 52,890-898.

Hart, E. et al. (2000). *Journal of Abnormal Child Psychology*, 28(3), 311.

Henze, D. et al. (2000). Dopamine Increases Excitability of Pyramidal Neurons in Primate Prefrontal Cortex. *Journal of Neurophysiology*, 84: 2799-2809.

Hobson, R & Lee, A. (1999). Imitation and identification in autism. *Journal of Child Psychology & Psychiatry & Allied Disciplines*, 40(4), 649-659.

Huffman, Huffman, & Vernoy (1994). *Psychology*, 3rd Ed. John Wiley & Sons, Inc.

Jancke, L., et al. (2000). *Cognitive Brain Research*, 10(1-2), 177-183.

Jolliffe, T. & Baron-Cohen, S. (1999). A test of central coherence theory: linguistic processing in high-functioning adults with autism or Asperger syndrome: is local coherence impaired? *Cognition*, 71(2), 149-185.

Karev, G. (2000). Cinema seating in right, mixed and left handers. *Cortex*, 36(5), 747-752

Kass, S. (1999). *APA Monitor*, 30(9).

Kastner, J., et al. (2000). The utility of reading to read with boys with ADHD-CT administered at two different intervals post methylphenidate ingestion. *Psychology in the Schools*, 37(4) 367-377.

Kaufman, J. & Charney, D. (2001). *Development & Psychopathology,* 13(3), 451-471.

Kern, L. et al. (2001). *Journal of Positive Behavior Interventions*, 3(1), 3-10.

Kircher, T. et al. (2001). Neuropsychologica 39(8), 798-809.

Koenen, K., et al. (2001). Measures of prefrontal system dysfunction in post-traumatic stress disorder. *Brain & Cognition*, 45(1), 64-78.

Koestner, Ryan, Bernieri, Holt, (1984) . Setting limits on children's behavior: The differential effects of controlling versus informational styles on intrinsic motivation and creativity. *Journal of Personality*, 52, 233-248.

Kovalenko, et al. (2000). Seasonal variations in internalizing, externalizing and substance use disorder in youth. *Psychiatry Research*, 94(2), 103-119.

Kubota, M et al. (2001). Alcohol consumption and frontal lobe shrinkage: study of 1432 non-alcoholic subjects. *Journal of Neurology, Neurosugery & Psychiatry*, 71(1), 104-106

Leekam, S., et al. (2000). Comparison of ICD-10 and Gilberg criteria for Asperger syndrome. *Autism*, 4(1) 11-28.

Leon, M. (2000). *Journal of Attention Disorders*, 4(1), 27-47.

Liechti, M., et al. (2001). Effects of MDMA on prepulse inhibition and habituation of startle in humans after pretreatment with citalopram, haloperidol or ketanserin. *Neuropsychopharmacology*. 24(3) 240-252.

Lundy, et al. (1999). Prenatal depression effects on neonates. *Infant Behavior Development*, 22(1), 119-129.

Lyvers, M. (2000). Cognition, emotion, and the alcohol-aggression relationship. *Experimental Clinical Psychopharmacology*, 8(4), 607-608.

Madden, et al. (1999). Aging and recognition memory: changes in regional cerebral blood flow associated with components of reaction time distributions. *Journal of Cognitive Neuroscience*, 11(5), 511- 520.

Mahoney J.(2000). Participation in school extracurricular activities as a moderator in the development of antisocial patterns. *Child Development*, 71 (2), 502-516.

Marston, H, et al (1999). *Psychopharmacology*.144(1) 67-76.

McEwen, B. & Magarinos, A. (2001). *Human Psychopharmacology Clinical & Experimental*, 16(1), S7-S19.

McEwen. (1999). *Annual Review of Neuroscience*, 22, 105-122.

Mednick, S. et al. (2002). The restorative effect of naps on perceptual deterioration. *Nature Neuroscience*, 5, 677-681.

Molina, et al. (1999). Interactive effects of ADHD and CD on early adolescent substance use. *Psychology Addictive Behaviors*, 13(4) 348 - 358.

Morgan, M. (1999). Memory deficits associated with recreational use of MDMA. *Psychopharmacology*. 141(1) 30-36.

Morgan, M. (2000). MDMA: A review of its possible persistent psychological effects. *Psychopharmacology*.152(3) 230-248.

Norvilitus, J. et al. (2000). Emotional appraisal in children with attention deficit/hyperactivity disorder and their parents. *Journal of Attention Disorders*, 4(1), 15-26.

Nunley, K. (2001). Layered Curriculum: The practical solution for teachers with more than one student in their classroom. Available through http://brains.org

O-Shea, E., et al.(1998). The relationship between the degree of neurodegeneration of rat brain 5-HT nerve terminals and the dose and frequency of administration of MDMA. *Neuropharmacology*, 37(7) 919-926.

O'Reilly, R. & Rudy,J. (2000). Computational principles of learning in the neocortex and hippocampus. *Hippocampus*, 10(4), 389-397.

Obrocki, J, et al. (1999). *British Journal of Psychiatry*. 175 186-188.

Ohnesorge, C. & Van Lancker, D. (2001). *Brain & Language*, 77(2), 135-165

Olff, (1999). Stress, depression and immunity: The role of defense and coping styles. *Psychiatry Research*, 85,1, 7-15.

Parrott, A. et al. (2000). Psychobiological problems in heavy ecstasy (MDMA) polydrug users. *Alcohol Dependence*, 60(1) 105-110.

Patrick, Skinner, & Connell, (1993). What motivates children's behavior and emotion? Joint effects of perceived control and autonomy in the academic domain. *Journal of Personality and Social Psychology*, 65, 781-791.

Pesta, B., Murphy, M., & Sanders, R. (2001). Are emotionally charged lures immune to false memory? *Journal of Experimental Psychology.: Learning, Memory & Cognition.* 27(2), 328-338.

Pickering, M. & Frisson, S. (2001). Processing ambiguous verbs: evidence from eye movements. *Journal of Experimental Psychology: Learning, Memory and Cognition.* 27(2), 556-573.

Pine, et al. (1999). *Journal of American Academy of child and Adolescent Psychiatry.* 38(3). 1024-1031.

Pinel, J. (1997). Biopsychology. 3rd ed. Allyn & Bacon, Needham Heights, MA.

Pugh, et. al. (2000). The angular gyrus in developmental dyslexia: Task-specific differences in functional connectivity in posterior cortex. *Psychological Science.* 11(1), 51-56.

Rahman, S. et al. (2001). Decision making and neuropsychiatry. *Trends in Cognitive Sciences,* 5(6), 271- 277.

Reeve, (1996). The interest-enjoyment distinction in intrinsic motivation. *Motivation and Emotion,* 13, 83-103

Reid Lyon, Ph.D, Chief of the Child Development and Behavior Branch of the Nat'l. Institute of Child Health and Human Development (NICHD). His presentation titled, "Reading Development, Difficulties and Intervention" was presented May 10, 2002 in Cambridge, MA

Reis, A. et al. (2001). Formal schooling influences two but not three dimensional naming skills. *Brain & Cognition*, 47(3), 397-411.

Reneman, L. (2000). Memory disturbances in "Ecstasy" users are correlated with an altered brain serotonin neurotransmission. *Psychopharmacology*.. 148(3) 322-324.

Rigby et al., (1992). Beyond the intrinsic-extrinsic dichotomy: Self-determination in motivation and learning. *Motivation and Emotion*, 16, 165-185.

Rumsey, et al., (1999). A functional lesion in developmental dyslexia: left angular gyral blood flow predicts severity. *Brain & Language,* 70(2), 187-204.

Schmidt, L. et al. (2001). Association of dopamine DRD4 with attention problems in normal childhood development. *Psychiatric Genetics*, 11(1), 25-29.

Schmolck, H & Squire, L. (2001). Impaired perception of facial emotions following bilateral damage to the anterior temporal lobe. *Neuropsychology*, 15(1), 30 - 38.

Schneider, R (2001). Training phonological skills and letter knowledge in children at risk for dyslexia: A comparison of three kindergarten intervention programs. *Journal of Educational Psychology*, 92,(2) 284-295.

Schultz, R., et al. (2000). Abnormal ventral temporal cortical activity during face discrimination among individuals with Autism and Asperger Syndrome. *Archives of General Psychiatry*, 57(4), 331-340.

Segal, N. (2000). Virtual Twins: New findings on within-family environmental influences on intelligence. *Journal of Educational Psychology*, 92 (3).442-448

Taylor & Dionee. (2000). Accessing Problem-solving strategy knowledge: The complementary use of concurrent verbal protocols and retrospective debriefing. *Journal of Educational Psychology*, 92 (3).413-425.

Shankaran, M. & Gudelsky, G. (1999). Involvement of the serotonin transporter in the formation of hydroxyl radicals induced by 3,4-MDMA. *Psychopharmacology*. 147(1) 66-72.

Shapira, (1976) . Expectancy determinants of intrinsically motivated behavior. *Journal of Personality and Social Psychology*, 34, 1235-1244.

Shaywitz, B. et al. (1998). Subtypes of reading disability: Variability around a phonological core. *Journal of Educational Psychology*, 90(3), 347-373.

Shepherd, G., editor. (1998). *The Synaptic Organization of the Brain.* Oxford University Press, Inc. New York.

Slotkin, T.; Seidler, F.; Ali, S. (2000). Cellular determinants of reduced adaptability of the aging brain: Neurotransmitter utilization and cell signaling responses after MDMA lesions, *Brain Research*, 879,(1-2) 163-173.

Small, S. et al. (2001). Circuit mechanisms underlying circuit encoding and retrieval in the long axis of the hippocampus formation. *Nature Neuroscience*, 4(4), 442-449.

Speck, O. et al. (2000). Gender differences in the functional organization of the brain for working memory. *Neuroreport*, 11(11), 2581-2585.

Stice, E. & Bearman, S. (2001). Body-Image and Eating Disturbances Prospectively Predict Increases in Depressive Symptoms in Adolescent Girls: A Growth Curve Analysis. *Developmental Psychology*, 37(5), 597-607.

Stice, E. et al. (2001). Relation of Early Menarche to Depression, Eating Disorders, Substance Abuse, and Comorbid Psychopathology Among Adolescent Girls. *Developmental Psychology*, 37(5), 608-619.

Stickgold, R., et. al. (2000). Visual discrimination learning requires sleep after training. *Nature Neuroscience* 3(12), 1237-1238.

Szatmari, P. et al. (2000). Autism: Long term outcome. *American. Journal of Psychiatry*, 157(12) 1980-1987.

Taffe, M., et al.(2001) Functional consequences of repeated (±)3,4-methylenedioxymethamphetamine (MDMA) treatment in rhesus monkeys *Neuropsychopharmacology*. 24(3) 230-239.

Tapert, S. et al. (2000) Alcohol affects teen brain, impairs memory. *National Institutes of Health News Release* Feb. 14.

Tucha, O. & Lange, K.(2001) Effects of methylphenidate on kinematic aspects of handwriting in hyperactive boys. *Journal of Abnormal Child Psychology*, 29(4), 351-356.

Tuchtenhagen, F., et al. (2000). High intensity dependence of auditory evoked dipole source activity indicates decreased serotonergic activity in abstinent ecstasy (MDMA) users *Neuropsychopharmacology*, 22(6) 608-617.

Valleran, Fortier, &Guay, (1997). Self-determination and persistence in a real-life setting: Toward a motivational model of high school dropout. *Journal of Personality and Social Psychology*, 72, 1161-1176.

Van Strien, J. & Van Beek. (2000). Ratings of emotion in laterally presented faces: Sex and handedness effects. *Brain & Cognition*, 44(3), 645-652.

Van Overschelde, J. & Healy, A. (2001). Learning of nondomain facts in high and low-knowledge domains. *Journal of Experimental Psychology: Learning, Memory, and Cognition,* 27(5), 1160-1171.

Verkes, R. et al. (2001) Cognitive performance and serotonergic function in users of ecstacy *Psychopharmacology,* 153(2), 196-202.

Vigliocco, G., et al (1999). Is "count" and "mass" information available when the noun is not? An investigation of tip of the tongue states and anomia *Journal of Memory and Language,* 40,(4) 534-558.

 Volkmar, F. et al, (2000) Asperger's Disorder. *American Journal of Psychiatry,* 157(2) 262-267.

Volkow, et al. (2000). Decreased brain dopamine activity with age is associated with impairment in frontal and cingulate metabolism. *American Journal of Psychiatry,* 157(1), 75-80

Waldie, K. & Mosley, J. (2000). Developmental trends in right hemispheric participation in reading. *Brain & Language.* 75(1), 108-122.

Weissman, D. & Banich, M. (2000). Cooperation between the cerebral hemispheres underlies the performance of complex but not simple tasks. *Neuropsychology,* 14, 41-59.

Wendt, P & Risberg, J. (2001). Ethanol reduces rCBF activation of left dorsolateral prefrontal cortex during a verbal fluency task, *Brain and Language, 77,* 197-215

Wolfson, A. (1998). Sleep schedules and daytime functioning in adolescents. *Child Development,* 69(4) 875-887.

Index